T0065803

I AM. . .

Seeing Yourself Through
the Eyes of God

David Mitchell, D.Min.
with
Robert L. Haines Jr., Ph.D.

WESTBOW
P R E S S®
A DIVISION OF THOMAS NELSON
& ZONDERVAN

WestBow Press books may be ordered through booksellers or by contacting:

WestBow Press
A Division of Thomas Nelson & Zondervan
1663 Liberty Drive
Bloomington, IN 47403
www.westbowpress.com
844-714-3454

ISBN: 978-1-6642-6429-8 (sc)
ISBN: 978-1-6642-6428-1 (hc)
ISBN: 978-1-6642-6430-4 (e)

Library of Congress Control Number: 2022906981

Print information available on the last page.

WestBow Press rev. date: 05/27/2022

CONTENTS

DEDICATION

This book is dedicated to my grandchildren: Milo, Owen, Rhett Caroline, Jackson, Vivian Rose, Taylor, and those to come. May you always know my love and find your true identity in Jesus Christ.

But we Christians have no veil over our faces; we can be mirrors that brightly reflect the glory of the Lord. And as the Spirit of the Lord works within us, we become more and more like him.

2 Corinthians 3:18, TLB

FOREWORD

There are only two families and two kingdoms in this world. Every person is in one or the other, and you can't be in both! When we enter by God's grace into His family, an amazing transformation takes place. We are someone we have never been before, and this new identity will never change! Understanding these vital truths changes everything in how we view ourselves, others, and our future.

There are few truths that the Enemy tries to hide from us more than the truths in this book. If he can keep us blinded here, we will live a sub-par spiritual life. Our past will shape our thinking and living before Christ. We will think that our prior life is WHO WE ARE when the exact opposite is true.

David Mitchell has done us all an incredible service. He has taken the profound truths about our identity in Christ and delivered them to us in a concise, simple, easily accessible way. This is a book that every believer must read and give to their friends! Christian parents should buy copies for their children and study it together.

You can't write these truths, as David has, unless you have experienced them. And every page of this book rings true because it is written by a godly leader who knows who he is in Christ. We are all indebted to Him!

By God's grace,

Bill Elliff
Founding and National Engage Pastor
The Summit Church, Arkansas

ACKNOWLEDGEMENTS

Oftentimes, it is not until we look back on our past that we can clearly see God's hand writing our future. For me, this is certainly the case. This book is the culmination of God using a lifetime of people to strengthen my ability, shape my beliefs, and provide a greater clarity of spiritual vision. I am eternally grateful for each relationship brought into my life by divine appointment.

My wife, Theresa, is truly God's blessing. Her gracious response to the pressure and time requirements being a pastor puts on a marriage and family can only be understood by her response to God's plan for her life. I am so grateful God brought a woman into my life who feels a portion of her answer to the question, "how would you describe yourself," is "I am called to be a pastor's wife." You are my greatest source of encouragement and self-confidence. Together, God blessed us with four wonderful children: Jill, Maggie, Luke, and Noah. I am also grateful for the loving spouses with which God has blessed our children. My favorite times are those rare occasions when we are all together.

What a privilege God has given me to serve with a multitude of Godly ministers on various church staffs. Ministering alongside you has made me a better pastor and leader. Chris McCarty, you have been an ever-present help in times of grammar trouble. Your willingness to read and reread chapters and give an honest opinion is invaluable. It is an honor to share ministry with Doug Fulton and Mark Parsley, two of the hardest working ministers on the planet. Your belief in the God-given vision of Mount Carmel and the joy you bring to our work environment is infectious. Thank you, Becky Cossey, for answering God's call on your life to be a ministry assistant.

Without the writing partnership of Bob Haines, this project would not have become a reality. When I mentioned, "I need help," you gladly agreed to assist. Your constant editorial advice and coaching is exactly the collaboration I needed. Thank you for your continual encouragement and relentless devotion of time. Thank you to your wife, Beverley, for sharing some of her time with you with me.

To my Mount Carmel family: You are a great expression of the body of Christ. You are a church family who is willing not only to hear from God but sacrificially put His vision into practice. You are unafraid of change and are boldly willing to go wherever God leads. You are a joy.

INTRODUCTION

For many years I did not see well, but I did not know it.

In my hometown, the question discussed at the coffee shop or the beauty shop was always the same: "What do you think this year's team will be like?" The "team" depended on the season of the year. With the same energy, enthusiasm, and excitement heard in the Hank Williams, Jr. (1996) song "Are You Ready For Some Football?" we would say, "Are you ready for some baseball," or "Are you ready for some basketball," or "Are you ready for some track?" You name the sport, yes, we were ready!

Although each sport was supported, one received more attention than the others. In our small town, girls' basketball was an all-consuming sport. Almost every year, our girls' high school basketball team was in competition for the state championship. This year was no exception: Once again, our girls were on their way to the capital city of Jackson to play in the 6,500-seat Mississippi Coliseum. It was there I realized I could not see.

Each year, our whole community strongly supported the girls' team. Families, friends, and neighbors convoyed the three hours to watch them compete. For many families, it was an annual tradition to book a block of hotel rooms and stay until they lost or won the championship game.

Like everyone else, my family was caught up in the excitement and enthusiasm. Unfortunately for my mom and brother, they were not able to make this year's trip. Fortunately for me, it was one of the rare occasions when it was only me and my dad. As we stepped into the coliseum, I was amazed by its size. My dad said, "Wonder what our girls thought when they walked out on this court for the first time?" We imagined their stomachs must have been swirling with butterflies considering, at maximum capacity, our gymnasium would seat a few hundred people, which was a far cry from over 6,000! After a quick stop by the concession stand, we located our friends and settled in for tipoff.

At the time, like many sporting centers today, the Mississippi Coliseum had one large scoreboard hanging in the center of the arena. As the game progressed, I would lean over and ask my dad, "What's the score?" He would tell me. Then I would ask, "How much time is left in this half?" He would tell me. Every few minutes, I would repeat this set of questions.

I never realized if he could read the scoreboard, I should also be able to see it. After the third round of this set of questions, my dad looked at me, somewhat surprised, and said, "The scoreboard is right there. It is as big as a car! Can't you see the score?" Without hesitation, I answered, "No, sir, I see the scoreboard, but I cannot see the score."

The next week, I was in the ophthalmologist's office for an eye exam. The eye doctor confirmed what the basketball game made evident: I could not see. It wasn't that I could not see at all; I could not see well at a distance. That day, I was fitted for my first of many pairs of glasses.

A week later, we went back to pick up my glasses. I was excited and nervous at the same time. I was nervous about wearing glasses all day every day and excited to see with clarity and new vison what I realized from the exam had been fuzzy for so many years.

My nerves disappeared when I walked out of the doctor's office. I saw plainly for the first time the way God intend my sight to be. I saw what I had not been able to see! Trees had leaves, animals were no longer a blur but had defined shapes, signs had letters, and clouds had distinct contours. I could see!

Glasses are a blessing to those whose sight needs improvement. They literally changed my life. My hope is this book will be a spiritual visual aid--"spiritual glasses," if you will--to help you see yourself through the eyes of God.

I believe you could be like me. You don't see well, but you are unaware your vision is distorted. Your vision is limited: not physically, but spiritually.

For many, when we begin to look at ourselves, and describe what we see, it is not what God intends. We see ourselves through the lens of the way life has shaped us rather than the vison God has of us. We need the corrective lens of God's word guided by His Holy Spirit to correct our vision.

You might ask, "What would be different about the way God sees me than the way I see myself?" Quite simply, God knows all there is to know about you. He knows you better than you know yourself. When God sees you, He sees you through the filter of His plans for you. His plans for you are significant. "'For I know the plans I have for you,' declares the LORD, 'plans to prosper you and not to harm you, plans to give you hope and a future'" (*New International Version Bible* [NIVB], 1973, Jeremiah 29:11).

For many of us, there is a significant difference in how we see ourselves and how God sees us. If asked to finish or complete the statement "**I am . . .**," what would you say? By default, you might answer, "I am a teacher," "I am a soldier," "I am retired," "I am a dad," "I am a wife," or "I am a teenager." All of these statements may be true, but if you could see yourself through the eyes of God, He would enable you to finish this statement in a completely different way.

The goal of this book is to convince you to complete the phrase "I am . . ." using the same language to describe yourself God would use. I am convinced that if I can convince you to see yourself through the eyes of God, the way He sees you, as a teenager, it will completely change the trajectory of your life; as a young adult, it will set you up for success; or as an older adult, it will give you an outward focus and purposeful excitement as you wake up every morning.

This book is written to encourage the person who cannot get away from the guilt of a 20-year-old bad decision. It is written to the person whose trust has been shattered, to the person who feels guilty because of a habit that cannot seem to be broken. It is written to people who have lost their reputation and to those who are broken-hearted.

It is also written because I believe on any given Sunday, in any individual church, behind many Sunday-morning faces, is a person who wants to keep the skeletons in the closet. Although we don't want our secrets to be known, we are desperate for hope, anxious for peace, and hungry for restoration.

Rather than reminding you of where you dropped the ball, the times you failed, how you sinned, or when you bungled it up, scripture tells us hope is found in seeing yourself as God sees you, and He does not see you as your failure or your past.

"For I know the plans I have for you," declares the Lord, *"plans to prosper you and not to harm you, plans to give you hope and a future."*

Jeremiah 29:11, NIVB

Seeing yourself through the eyes of God, the way God intends your sight to be moves you from living your life to accomplish a task to living a life of focused purpose. When you see yourself through the eyes of God, you live through the identity God has given you. It also changes your response to the phrase, "I am . . ." Please, join me on a journey to discover a completely new God-given self-identity.

NOTES

CHAPTER 1

I Am Chosen

I Am Chosen

Norman was blind. He was not born blind, but in the life he lived before he became a Christian, diabetes mixed with alcohol and drugs took his sight. Although he could not see, he was an exceptional guitar player and had a voice that drew you in like a warm cup of coffee on a cold, cloudy morning. After giving his life to Christ, it was natural for to him to use his musical ability to tell the story of how Jesus completely changed his life and restored his sight: not physically but spiritually.

One thing I regret about our friendship was he did not live close enough to regularly attend the church I was pastoring. However, I did frequently invite him to sing in our services. He was not only a terrific singer, but he had an extremely quick wit and always wore a wide smile that complemented his dynamic personality.

One Sunday, I scheduled Norman to sing. Before the service began, we were talking like old friends who had not seen each other for a long time. It was our routine on those fortunate days to joke around and enjoy each other's company before he would sing for our congregation.

I don't know why, but for some reason on this particular Sunday our light-hearted jokes turned to a more serious discussion. I said, "Norman, because I never knew you when you could see, there is something I want to tell you that is critical to our friendship."

He said, "We know each other pretty well, but if there is something you can tell me that will make our friendship stronger, I want to know about it."

I said, "This is so important to me because I could easily describe you so well to someone else that they could pick you out of a crowd. But you have never seen me." With my most serious pastor's voice, I said,

"Norman, do you believe when we get to heaven we will receive new bodies?"

"Yes," he said.

"So when you get to heaven you will not have diabetes?" I asked.

He replied, "Yes," once again.

"You also will have your sight restored?"

"Yes."

I continued, "because the Bible says in heaven we will be known as we are known on Earth, and because you will have your sight restored when we get to heaven, I want you to be able to recognize me. So, let me describe myself. That way, you can paint a picture of me in your mind by my description. I am 6' 4" tall, with thick, wavy, blond hair, and deep blue eyes. I have about a 44-inch chest and a 34-inch waist."

Without hesitation, Norman quickly said, "Preacher, it ain't a sin to be blind--but it is to lie . . . especially in church . . . and especially just before you preach."

And Norman was right! With dress shoes, I might top out at 5' 8", my waist and chest numbers are almost identical, and male pattern baldness has plagued my family for generations. Without ever seeing me, he knew my description of myself was less than honest.

How about you? How would you describe yourself? How would you finish this statement?

"I am . . ."

I Am...

This book is about focusing on your identity--to help you recognize the dramatic difference in the way many people see themselves versus how God sees them. It is written to motivate you to abandon living life through your self-identity and to begin living in the power and significance of seeing yourself through God's eyes. In the following chapters, you will find help to live in the power found in discovering your true identity as a believer in Jesus. You will be confronted with numerous opportunities to explore the truth of scripture that reveals how God sees you. Once the Holy Spirit convinces you to see yourself through the eyes of God, your entire outlook on life will change. Through that discovery, you will find liberty, victory, and freedom to live your life through the lens of how God sees you and who you are in His sight.

Understanding How God Looks at You

If you are a Christian, God's Word describes you beautifully:

"But you are a chosen people, a royal priesthood, a holy nation, God's special possession, that you may declare the praises of him who called you out of darkness into his wonderful light" (*NIVB*, 1973, 1 Peter 2:9).

No matter how you see yourself, God sees you as far more precious than you could ever dream or imagine possible.

God sees you as chosen. Any time you are chosen for something, no matter how small or insignificant it might be, it is lifegiving. It doesn't matter whether you are being chosen for dodgeball in the sixth grade, gaining entrance into college as a high school senior, or being asked to marry your high school sweetheart as a young adult, there is something inspiring and reassuring about being chosen.

*But you are a chosen people,
a royal priesthood, a holy nation,
God's special possession, that you
may declare the praises of him who
called you out of darkness into his
wonderful light.*

1 Peter 2:9, NIVB

As important as those events in life may be, they are all insignificant when compared to being chosen by God. Before the foundation of the world, He chose you to be a recipient of His royal love.

"Long ago, even before he made the world, God chose us to be his very own through what Christ would do for us" (*The Living Bible*, 1971, Eph. 1:4).

Being Chosen

Each year at the end of the college football season, professional teams decide who they will choose to join their individual teams through the National Football League's draft process. In 2021, with protocols for limited attendance, more than 160,000 people crowded into the city of Cleveland, Ohio, to see who would be chosen for the draft (Associated Press, 2021); another 6.1 million viewers watched at home to see who would be picked (Around the NFL Staff, 2021).

The number one choice was Trevor Lawrence, quarterback from Clemson, chosen by the Jacksonville Jaguars (NFL.com, n.d.).

Teams in the National Basketball Association also choose the players they would like to join their organizations. Their number one pick in 2021 was Cade Cunningham from Oklahoma State, chosen by the Detroit Pistons (NBA.com Staff, 2021).

Major League Baseball chooses players in the same manner. The number one choice in the 2021 draft was Henry Davis, a catcher from Louisville, who was chosen by the Pittsburg Pirates (Callis & Mayo, 2021).

As exciting and fulfilling as it would be to be chosen by a professional sports team, you have been chosen for a more valuable purpose. You are God's number one choice. You will never be traded, dropped, or retired. God chose you, selected you, adopted you, and saved you to be in an eternal relationship with Him.

Sometimes I hear someone say, "God may have chosen other people, but because of the things I have done, the places I have been, the way I have messed up, the hurt I have caused, and the mistakes I have made, He would never choose me." As hard as it may be to believe, no matter where your life's path has taken you, He did choose you to be His own. Yes, He would; yes, He does; and yes, He has chosen you.

When you start to see yourself the way God sees you, you will begin to realize the joy of knowing He not only chose you, but He changed your status. When God chose you, he chose you to be his royal representative:

"But you are a chosen people, a royal priesthood" (*NIVB*, 1973, 1 Peter 2:9).

You Are a Royal Representative

When scripture says you are a part of His royal priesthood, it means you are to represent King Jesus; God chose you to be His representative. Living like a member of His royal family is your responsibility. As a member of His royal priesthood, you have the privilege of speaking to and hearing from God. You have free access to His presence at any time you would like.

The Spirit himself testifies with our spirit that we are God's children. Now if we are children, then we are heirs--heirs of God and co-heirs with Christ.

Romans 8:16-17, NIVB

Often when we hear the word *royalty*, we think of the royal family of the House of Windsor: the reigning royal house of the United Kingdom and the other Commonwealth realms. But what does it mean to be a royal representative? Quite simply, *being royal* means you have a family connection--a blood connection--to a king.

That's why, when God chose to describe you, He called you His royal representative (*NIVB*, 1973). Imagine how significant God must see you if He describes you as His representative. When you become a Christian, you have the right to be His royal representative because you have been adopted into His royal family. You are a member of His holy family through the blood of Jesus and by status.

Paul described your adoption this way:

"The Spirit himself testifies with our spirit that we are God's children. Now if we are children, then we are heirs--heirs of God and co-heirs with Christ" (*NIVB*, 1973, Romans 8:16-17).

How Did You Become Holy?

The word *holy* is a descriptive designation of a characteristic. When we say something is holy, it means it is dedicated for a particular purpose. You have been chosen, or dedicated, for the particular purpose of being God's royal representative as a member of His holy family. That means God set you apart for a particular purpose. God chose you to be His representative and to be devoted to Him exclusively. You are holy because scripture says you are holy, not because of anything you have done. God is holy, and whatever God's word says is holy *is* holy.

"You are God's number one choice. You will never be traded, dropped, or retired."

As Americans, we live in a republic. Nations who have a king live under the reign of a monarchy. Others live under the rule of an aristocracy, and unfortunately, some people live under the reign of a dictatorship. Because you are in God's royal family, you live in a theocracy. A theocracy is a system of government by divine guidance, or ruled in the name of God (Merriam-Webster, n.d.-c). That means God is King of His kingdom. It also means He has selected you to be part of His holy royal family. In His kingdom, you are dedicated for His purpose, set apart to represent Him as a holy citizen under His rule.

If you are still not convinced to see yourself through the eyes of God, scripture also tells us you are His special possession. All the earth is God's possession--including you.

"The heavens are Yours, the earth also is Yours; The world and all it contains, You have established them" (*New American Standard Bible* [NASB], 1960, Psalm 89:11).

You can see yourself through your own eyes. You can also see yourself through the eyes of your enemy. Most importantly, you can see yourself through the eyes of God. Fortunately, regardless of how you see yourself or how your enemy sees you, it does not change who you are; you are God's highly valued, special possession!

When we begin to see ourselves the way God sees us, it changes everything about how we live our lives. God doesn't modify our behavior to change us. He changes us to modify our behavior. When you begin to see yourself as chosen by God, a part of His royal family, and His special possession, you will begin to see purpose in your daily work. You will also be motivated to be a better spouse and to be a more loving parent. When you see yourself as chosen, living the Christian life is becoming what you already are in Christ.

Revisiting Norman

It is difficult for me to describe Norman the way I last saw him. Not only was he blind, but he had also lost several toes, part of one leg, and the ends of three fingers. If you did not know him, based on his outward appearance, you would wonder what a person like this has to live for.

In typical Norman fashion, the night before his leg was amputated, he asked his wife to bring some music to the hospital room for a final dance. "I want to celebrate with my wife, the love of my life, in one final dance. I want to thank my Savior who gave His life to save me despite the way I lived before becoming a Christian."

Norman and Sandy Beard

Norman never saw himself as being punished by God. He saw himself as changed by Jesus. Norman looked forward to going home to heaven, where he would get a new body, and being able to see his heavenly Father with new eyes. Shortly after I last saw him, he went home to heaven. One day, when I join him in heaven, he will see me with his new eyes--for the very first time.

Just like Norman, no matter how you see yourself, you have been selected by the Savior, you are favored by the Father, and you are holy and without blame in God's sight. God sees you as you really are: more important than you could ever imagine.

"For we are God's handiwork, created in Christ Jesus" (*NIVB*, 1973, Eph. 2:10).

#iamchosen

For we are God's handiwork,
created in Christ Jesus.

Ephesians 2:10, NIVB

NOTES

CHAPTER 2

I Am Forgiven

I Am Forgiven

Do you have a favorite "knock-knock" joke? Some of my favorites are:

Knock! Knock!
Who's there?
Eyesore.
Eyesore who?
Eyesore do love you!

Knock! Knock!
Who's there?
A broken pencil.
A broken pencil who?
Never mind, it's pointless.

Knock! Knock!
Who's there?
An extraterrestrial.
An extraterrestrial who?
Wait . . . how many extraterrestrials do you know?

My all-time favorite "knock-knock" joke is:

Knock! kKnock!
Who's there?
Mustache.
Mustache who?
I mustache you a question, but I will shave it for later.

While we may enjoy a good knock-knock joke, the question this book is asking is no joke and cannot wait until later. The question is this: How can you see yourself through the eyes of God?

How Does God See You?

As we are discovering, there are many ways God sees you. One of the most liberating ways in which He sees you is forgiven. God sees you as completely, totally, fully, forever, wholly, and entirely forgiven.

"As distant as the East is from the West, that is how far He has removed our sins from us" (*International Standard Version Bible*, 2014, Psalm 103:12).

It is important to know you did not earn His forgiveness, and there is no means you have that could allow you to purchase it. His forgiveness is offered not because of anything you have done. It is all because of the resources He has expended to prove His love for you.

"In Him we have redemption through His blood, the forgiveness of sins, according to the riches of God's grace" (*NIVB*, 1973, Ephesians 1:7).

God passionately wants you to discover your identity as forgiven. He spent all of eternity organizing history so you might discover this one truth.

"God's eternal power and character cannot be seen. But from the beginning of creation, God has shown what these are like by all He has made" (*Contemporary English Version Bible*, 1995, Romans 1:20).

Making sure His forgiveness is not hidden, He inspired authors to paint word pictures in scripture of countless examples of people with baggage just like yours whose lives were forever altered when they discovered their real identity as forgiven.

He is the atoning sacrifice for our sins, and not only for ours but also for the sins of the whole world.

1 John 2:2, NIVB

Driving an exclamation point into the bedrock of salvation history, God sent His son, Jesus, to live a perfect life and be offered as a perfect sacrifice so we can have complete forgiveness.

"He is the atoning sacrifice for our sins, and not only for ours but also for the sins of the whole world" (*NIVB*, 1973, 1 John 2:2).

Struggling With Forgiveness

We normally think of forgiveness in two ways: forgiveness being extended or forgiveness being received. However, both extending and receiving forgiveness can be challenging.

Almost all of us find it hard to extend forgiveness. For instance, it is difficult to forgive someone who posts something unflattering (or worse, untrue) about you on social media. It is tough to forgive the teacher who seems to be unfair. It is challenging to forgive the spouse who has caused unforgettable pain. It is also hard to forgive the parent who said something hurtful about us when we were young.

Those who have experienced the forgiveness of Jesus will tell you that until you know His forgiveness, it is impossible to completely offer your forgiveness to others. Until you encounter the grace, acceptance, and mercy of God's forgiveness, you have no basis from which to offer forgiveness. Only experiencing the forgiveness of God allows you the knowledge necessary to offer true forgiveness.

As difficult as it may be to extend forgiveness in these circumstances, life's failures and mistakes can haunt our memories in ways that make receiving forgiveness feel even more impossible. Like looking out across the ocean and knowing you could never swim to the other side, receiving forgiveness can seem like an experience you will never know.

If anyone is in Christ, the new creation has come: The old has gone, the new is here!

2 Corinthians 5:17, NIVB

Struggling With Guilt

Many times, we struggle to feel worthy of receiving God's forgiveness. This struggle is frequently because we know we are guilty. The weight of our sin seems so heavy we feel it impossible to believe God could, or would, forgive us. This mindset of guilt makes receiving forgiveness seem out of reach. Knowing we are guilty and in need of God's forgiveness can be a barrier that keeps us from seeing ourselves as worthy of being forgiven.

For many people, the way they see themselves and the way God sees them is very different. When God sees you, He not only sees you as worthy of being forgiven, but (for the Christian) He sees you as already forgiven. Once you become a Christian, you begin to understand and recognize that where you are overcomes where you have been. Where you are (forgiven) overcomes where you have been (guilty). Remember what Ephesians 1:7 says: "In Him we have redemption . . . the forgiveness of sins" (*NIVB*, 1973).

When you become a Christian, the feeling of being guilt-ridden is replaced with knowing you have been completely forgiven. In Paul's second letter to the believers in Corinth, he stated it this way:

"If anyone is in Christ, the new creation has come: The old has gone, the new is here!" (*NIVB*, 1973, 2 Cor. 5:17).

God not only forgives you, but He gives you the ability to see yourself as forgiven. When you are saved and understand you are forgiven, you start to live your new identity.

"One of the most liberating ways in which He sees you is forgiven. God sees you as completely, totally, fully, forever, wholly, and entirely forgiven."

What Is Your Identity?

The movie *Overcomer* (Kendrick, 2019) is filled with characters who struggle with the challenges their lives' circumstances have on their identities. The beginning of the movie shows a news story of the town's mill closing, leaving a town full of workers who lose their manufacturing jobs along with their identities as mill workers. The lead character is a basketball coach who is no longer known as a basketball coach because he has no team to coach. He is then asked to coach the cross-country team, an activity he says, "is not even a real sport." The only person to show up for tryouts is a girl with asthma. We are then introduced to a man who abandons his daughter when she is a baby. We also watch as a husband and wife struggle in their marriage. All of these struggles can be seen around us, on the news, or in our own lives.

The Kendrick brothers, Stephen and Alex, who wrote the script along with BelleNur, said they wrote it to help people answer the question posed in the film's tagline: "What do you allow to define you?" (IMDb, 2019). *Overcomer* forces audiences to wrestle with the question of how to live life when all you have to live from is your identity in Christ. This topic is further addressed in a Women of Faith blog:

https://www.womenoffaith.com/blog/
what-do-you-allow-to-define-you

"If all you have to live from is your identity as forgiven by the King of Kings, you have all you need to live a happy and productive life."

Alex Kendrick, also the lead actor in the film (as cited in Carpenter, n.d.), said:

> It's interesting that our culture is debating who gets to define what our identity should be . . . Culture would say it's your feelings or at least it's your status, your title, or your finances. Because God created us, we would say that the creator gets to define His creation and that we find the fullest intended version of ourselves when we find ourselves in the one who created us. What we say in the movie is God loves you the most, knows you the best, and has the authority to tell you who you are. (para. 5)

If all you have to live from is your identity as forgiven by the King of Kings, you have all you need to live a happy and productive life. God's resounding message from scripture repeatedly tells us this: Those who place their trust in Him as their savior are forever and always forgiven. God says, "I will forgive their iniquity, and I will remember their sins no more" (*English Standard Version Bible* [ESVB], 2001, Jeremiah 31:34). No matter how you have allowed culture to define you, or how you have defined yourself, the only definition that matters is the one God has for you, which is forgiven.

God's offer of forgiveness is unique in that it involves setting us free from the trap, influence, and impact of sin. We identify with the struggle of the Apostle Paul when he says, "Wretched man that I am! Who will set me free from the body of this death?" (*NASB*, 1960, Romans 7:24). God offers us forgiveness through the death and sacrifice of Jesus, which provides the opportunity to be set free from the penalty of death.

The Benefits of Being Forgiven

When you are forgiven, God works in your life to make you more like Him. He begins to mold you and change you into the image of a forgiven person the moment you trust Jesus as your savior. God's word tells us that very thing:

> I will give you a new heart, and put a new spirit within you; and I will remove the heart of stone from your flesh and give you a heart of flesh. And I will put My Spirit within you and bring it about that you walk in My statutes, and are careful and follow My ordinances. (*ESVB*, 2001, Ezekiel 36:26-27)

To allow God to mold us into His image requires considerable change for everyone. Although God sees us as forgiven, we have to agree to let Him make the changes He desires in our lives. When we prohibit Him from conforming us to His likeness, we are hindering our abilities to live in His plan for our lives.

Resisting Change

To be honest, there are some areas of my life where I am never going to change. For example, I will never order cheese on a hamburger. When ordering at a drive-thru restaurant, sometimes your order can be misunderstood. So, when the waitress says "What else can I get for you?" and I say, "Nothing," and they say, "Is the order on your screen correct," I say, "Yes, but more importantly, is the order on *your* screen correct? I said, 'no cheese, please.'"

Even with this clarity, the last time I ordered a hamburger and specified no cheese, when I opened the wrapper, it had not one slice, but *two* slices of smelly, gooey, runny, yellow cheese melted into both of the now-desecrated 100% beef patties. Once a burger has been "cheesed," it is like a wedding. The two become one, and what cheese has joined together can never be put asunder!

Because this was not the first time my hamburger had been violated by cheese, I checked my order before leaving the drive-thru window. On this occasion, the waitress noticed I did not drive away to cheeseburger paradise. She cautiously opened the window and kindly asked, "Can I get you something else?" I answered, "Yes, I said 'No cheese, please.' This burger not only has cheese, I think it must have extra cheese." She responded, "Oh, sir, I am so sorry! I thought you said 'mo' cheese!'"

God Changes Everyone

Another area of my life I never plan to change is in the area of cats. Many people like cats, but they are not my favorite, to say the least. People will often try to change my mind about this. Some of the time, this happens when someone shows me a video of a cat playing with a string.

It doesn't move me.

Another cat lover said, "Watch this video of these kittens; you will just love them."

I didn't.

Still trying to change my opinion, another feline fanatic brought me an article with a story about a cat that saved its family. Still unimpressed, I can only say cats will never be on my top ten list.

Just as I have taken a "no-change oath" related to cheeseburgers and cats, some have taken a no-change position spiritually. It isn't that they do not desire for God to make changes to their circumstances. Instead, they do not want God to change *them*.

We may not allow God to change us into His image, but there are things we are more than happy for God to change. We may desire the change so strongly we ask Him to make the change for us. We find ourselves praying, "God, will you change my problems, will you meet my needs, will you modify my child's attitude, will you improve my revenue stream, or will you change my husband or wife?" However, for our circumstances to change, we have to allow God to change us.

The good news is, if you are a believer, God has already changed you. He has changed you from guilty to forgiven. As forgiven, you can begin to live in the liberty of your new distinctiveness. The more you allow God to change you into His image, the more your circumstances will change.

An Example of True Forgiveness

In the Gospel of John, Chapter 8, we meet a woman who wishes her circumstances would change (*NIVB*, 1973). The Bible says it was early morning and Jesus was at the temple teaching. A large crowd had gathered to hear Him. As He began to teach, the religious leaders of the day forcibly brought the woman and made her stand before the crowd and Jesus. They said, "Teacher, this woman was caught in the act of adultery" (*NIVB*, 1973, John 8:4). While this is still a serious offense today, in the time when this was written, the penalty for adultery was stoning. Therefore, this accusation--and its outcome--was literally a matter of life and death!

As we continue reading the story, the image that comes to my mind is as if the crowd and all the accusers have disappeared.

> He stood up and said to them, "Let him who is without sin among you be the first to throw a stone at her." And once more he bent down and wrote on the ground. But when they heard it, they went away one by one, beginning with the older ones, and Jesus was left alone with the woman standing before him. (*ESVB*, 2001, John 8:7-9)

The woman is alone with Jesus when He asks her, "'Has no one condemned you?' She said, 'No one, Lord.' And Jesus said, 'Neither do I condemn you; go, and from now on sin no more'" (*ESVB*, 2001, John 8:10-11). Just moments before, in the eyes of everyone there, including in her own mind, she was condemned to death. However, when Jesus spoke, forgiveness came, and her circumstances completely changed.

Imagine if your most secret sin was announced publicly to everyone you know--those things you want no one to know. Imagine if it was brought to God's attention by those who would like for you to be embarrassed, as those who brought this woman before Jesus wanted her to be. Fortunately, your friends and neighbors may never know your secret sins, but Jesus already does. However, His response is the same today as it was on the day John wrote about, and the same to you as it was to this woman. He offers forgiveness, not condemnation.

When you are forgiven, you become a different person. As Christians, we have new identities in Christ. No longer is the Christian a captive to sin and death!

I think we all like the idea of being forgiven. The hard part is allowing God to change us into people who live like we are forgiven. Finding

I Am...

your identity as forgiven by the one who created you has the potential to change your entire perspective on every aspect of life.

The forgiveness you need to change, win, live in victory, go forward, face adversity, and overcome guilt, doubt, and conviction is already yours. See yourself as God's sees you--forgiven--and live in His great freedom.

Knock, knock!
Who's there?
Forgiven.
Forgiven who?
Forgiven you! That's who.

#iamforgiven

NOTES

CHAPTER 3

I Am Redeemed

I Am Redeemed

It was a clock radio.

We all have things on our wish lists, and at the top of mine was a clock radio. You would not have been impressed by its appearance. It was small: about 10 inches long, 5 inches wide, and 4 inches tall. The top and sides were pure white, and the front was one solid piece of clear plastic. I know it doesn't seem like a lofty wish, but at the time it was so far out of my reach it could have been a Rolls Royce or a Lamborghini.

A part of this clock's appeal was the way it displayed time. Behind the clear plastic front were the numbers displaying the time. The time was displayed in a digital format but not electronic. The numbers were held by barriers, somewhat like a deck of cards. Each number had two rigs holding them from the top. When the minute or the hour changed, the number would be released from the top, revealing the time. If you have seen the movie Groundhog Day, you have a good idea of this clock's appearance. The main attraction for me was the clock's dual purpose: It was also a radio.

As a child with no job and no allowance, it seemed my wish would never become reality. Sitting on the couch in our living room, somewhat disheartened, thinking how far out of reach the clock radio was, I noticed a catalog. Out of boredom, I picked it up and uninterestedly began to thumb through. To my surprise, there it was--an advertisement for the exact clock radio I so badly longed. The impossible had just become possible! Why? Because this was not an ordinary catalog--it was the S&H Green Stamps catalog. The reason this unique catalog made the impossible possible was *nothing in the catalog was for sale.*

On the front was a happy "Leave It to Beaver"-type family, excitedly looking at the catalog painted in Norman Rockwell-style pastels. The Green Stamps catalog was like a Christmas wish catalog with sections for men, women, children, and home. Because nothing in the catalog was for sale, the only way to obtain something from the catalog was to redeem it with Green Stamps.

Green Stamps worked like grocery store customer loyalty or reward cards, but instead of discounting the price of your purchase, you were given Green Stamps. The stamps were saved, put into a Quick Saver Book, and then redeemed for your choice of product from the catalog. The more money you spent in stores that gave the stamps, the more stamps you received. If you saved more stamps, you could redeem them for items of greater value. To redeem the clock radio, nine books of stamps were needed.

I explained to my mother how badly I wanted the clock radio. Realizing she had the opportunity to help her child have one of his wishes granted, she agreed to let me have the Green Stamps from her purchases at the grocery store. Each time she went to the store, I anxiously took the stamps and put them in the Quick Saver Book. It took months of saving, but eventually I saved the necessary nine Green Stamps books. What a happy day when the impossible became possible and I presented my Green Stamps to redeem the clock radio!

What Does It Mean to be Redeemed?

When is the last time you redeemed something? If asked to complete the statement "I am . . ." with one word that best described you, you probably would not say "redeemed." One reason may be that redeemed is a word we do not use often or much less use to describe ourselves. But when God sees you, He sees you as redeemed.

Knowing He wanted more than anything to redeem you, God made a plan for your redemption. Fully understanding the cost, He continued to move forward with His redemption plan. The Old Testament prophet Isaiah says it this way: "Fear not, for I have redeemed you; I have called you by name, you are mine" (*ESVB*, 2001, Isaiah 43:1). We are learning that because of God's great love for us, He sees us in many ways, and one of those ways is worthy of redemption.

You seldom hear the word redeemed unless you are in a church service. It is a "churchy" word like propitiation, imputation, edification, or sanctification. These are words you could hear in a sermon that sound important but, for the most part, are unsure of their meaning.

Because God sees you as redeemed, wrapping your mind around a clear understanding of the word can deeply change the way you see yourself.

Redemption is, in essence, an exchange. Something of value is exchanged for something of an even greater value by the redeemer. God exchanged His son to redeem you. God thought you more valuable than His son's life.

When God sees you, He so desires to have a relationship with you that He sees you as worthy of orchestrating salvation history so He might redeem you. The Apostle Paul described redeemed this way: "Our great God and Savior Jesus Christ . . . gave himself for us to redeem us . . . and to purify for himself a people that are His very own" (*NIVB*, 1973, Titus 2:13-14). We were held captive by sin, and the ransom for our redemption was paid from God's wealth through His son, Jesus.

In scripture, redeem means to, "pay the price required to secure the release of a convicted criminal" (Butler, 1991, p. 1170). Because of our sin, we are all convicted, guilty, and sentenced to pay a debt beyond our means. According to Romans 6:23, the debt we owe is death: "for the wages of sin is death" (NIVB, 1973). Through the death of Jesus, God paid the necessary price for our redemption.

God Can Redeem Anyone

The book of Titus was written to people who lived on an island called Crete. Epimenides, known as one of the seven wise poets of ancient Greece, is quoted by Paul in Titus when he described the reputation of the Cretans: "One of the Cretans, a prophet of their own, said, 'Cretans are always liars, evil beasts, lazy gluttons'" (*ESVB*, 2001, Titus 1:12). If this is the opinion the Cretans had of themselves, to say the people of Crete had low self-value is an understatement.

Crete was the Las Vegas of Paul's day. They might have been the originators of the statement, "What happens on Crete stays on Crete." The culture in which they lived, and the mindset of the Cretans, affected them in such a way that they saw themselves as anything but worthy of being redeemed.

In his letter to Titus, Paul told the Christians living on Crete they needed to see themselves as God saw them . . . as redeemed. He was helping them see they were not the way Epimenides or anyone else says they are. They are God's own possession, redeemed by Jesus's blood.

Just as God paid the debt to redeem the Cretans and make them His own possession, He has done the same for you. The price required for your redemption is so high that God is the only one with the resources to pay it. You are also valuable because Jesus's death and blood is the currency used to redeem you.

"The price required for your redemption is so high God is the only one with the resources to pay it."

The Price Paid for Your Redemption

Have you seen History Channel's television show *Pawn Stars*? It is a reality television show about a pawn shop in Las Vegas. Rick Harrison, who owns the pawn shop, says in the opening narration the most amazing thing about the pawn shop is, "you never know what is going to come through these doors" (2012-2019). And he is right: Some of the items people have brought to the pawn shop are a buoy signed by "The Hoff" (David Hasselhoff), the car used in the *Wayne's World* movie, dinosaur eggs, and a giant Super Mario Brothers *Mario* statue.

Many items brought into the pawn shop make you wonder why people would consider pawning or selling something of such sentimental value--family heirlooms like mother's engagement ring, grandfather's gold pocket watch, or great-great-great-grandfather's Civil War uniform.

Let's imagine you pawn your mother's engagement ring. You spend a sleepless night waiting for the pawn shop to open because you realize the ring is far more valuable to you than the cash they paid you. You recognize you made a monumental mistake. The next day, you are there when the doors open.

Anxiously, you ask if they still have your ring. Heaven must be on your side because, yes, they still have it in their jewelry case. You tell them you would like your ring back, and they gladly offer it to you--for 50% more than they paid you for it! Willingly, you pay their price because no price is too high to buy back what is invaluable to you.

What does a pawn shop have to do with God? Well, God sees you as priceless. Demonstrating this truth, He paid the highest price possible to have a relationship with you. "Our great God and Savior Jesus . . .

gave himself for us to redeem us" (*ESVB*, 2001, Titus 2:13-14). This means you are so valuable the only price high enough to redeem you was God's son Jesus. He was the price paid for your redemption.

One of the best things about God's redemption is it is not available to a limited audience: God, "who gave Himself for *us* to redeem *us* [emphasis added]," means you are included in the "us" (*ESVB*, 2001, Titus 2:14). Scripture repeatedly uses the word "whosoever" to talk about those God is willing to redeem. Examples include: "Whosoever will lose his life for my sake shall find it" (*King James Bible* [KJB], 1611/1987, Matthew 16:25); "Whosoever shall call upon the name of the Lord shall be saved" (*KJB*, 1611/1987, Romans 10:13); "For God so loved the world, that he gave his only begotten Son, that whosoever believeth in him should not perish, but have everlasting life" (*KJB*, 1611/1987, John 3:16). These passages provide evidence that whoever will lose his life, call on the Lord, and believe in Jesus, will be redeemed by God.

Why is God willing to pay such a high price for your redemption? Because there is no other way to find freedom from the constant pull of sin. No matter how hard we try, we cannot free ourselves from sin's grip. Paul describes being set free this way:

> For when you were slaves of sin, you were free in regard to righteousness. But what fruit were you getting at that time from the things of which you are now ashamed? For the end of those things is death. But now that you have been set free from sin and have become slaves of God, the fruit you get leads to sanctification and its end, eternal life. For the wages of sin is death, but the free gift of God is eternal life in Christ Jesus our Lord. (*ESVB*, 2001, Romans 6:20-23)

*For the wages of sin is death, but
the free gift of God is eternal life in
Christ Jesus our Lord.*

Romans 6:23, ESVB

Easter Ducks?

During my lifetime, I've had some unusual pets. Maybe you had some of the normal pets of childhood like cats, dogs, horses, or even a really mean Shetland pony. I had all of those, as well. However, some of my unusual pets were a blue-and-yellow macaw, an owl, love birds, rabbits, and Easter ducks.

In an unusual move, without any request from me, one Easter my parents thought (instead of chocolate rabbits) it would be a great idea to give me live baby Easter ducks. The first time I saw these Easter ducks, they were small balls of waddling, quacking, yellow fur. If you needed a smile, they were the perfect prescription. When I first met them, it seemed like a relationship made in heaven.

Early on, my parents and I went out of our way to make sure they had all the comforts of "duck life" a duck could ever imagine. They even had their own duck house. Not just any duck house, but a two-story duck mansion with its own duck swimming pool.

Quickly, these small balls of yellow fur began to grow. They matured into full-grown, very large, white adult ducks. Like many living gifts that seem fun at the time and, in the mind of the giver, hold a dream of bringing long-term enjoyment, in the end, having Easter ducks as pets became a nightmare. What was intended to bring pleasure became a constant annoyance.

Although these were Easter ducks and not Easter rabbits, they began to multiply. The duck swimming pool turned into a smelly, green cesspool. The duck mansion deteriorated into a rundown, overcrowded candidate for a home makeover show on HGTV™.

Not only was their living environment a smelly eyesore, it seems, at some point, the ducks lost their identity and began to see themselves as people. With their new identities, they were no longer happy with the duck life. They wanted to live as people rather than ducks. They made it plain that they wanted to leave the now-dilapidated duck mansion and slimy duck pool--and move into our house!

Their plan of attack all day, every day, was to stand on the back porch of our home and peck on the sliding glass door. Anytime anyone tried to go out or come in those doors, the ducks would work like a well-organized team to get at least one member of their team into the house. Because they spent most of the day standing on the back porch trying to come into the house, the back porch became a minefield of duck poo. They were trying to live in an environment and a life they were never created to have.

Finally, my parents decided they had all the enjoyment from the Easter ducks they could stand. Getting rid of an unwanted, full-grown, spoiled, adult duck is like trying to throw away a garbage can you no longer use. It is almost impossible to find someone willing to take it away.

After exhausting almost all of our contacts, we finally found a friend with a farm who agreed to let the ducks have a new home on their pond. I still remember the day we set the ducks free. I thought, "They will never be happy here; they will not get out of the truck and, if they do, they will follow us all the way home."

Sadly, I opened the doors of the truck, reluctantly preparing to force them out. Much to my surprise, it was as if they had never met us. They immediately forgot about the duck mansion, the swimming pool, and trying to invade our home. They had been set free. They found something they had been longing for but did not know existed.

When we released them and they saw the pond, I watched the saying, "they took to it like a duck takes to water," come to life. They had been

For I know that my Redeemer lives,
and at the last he will stand upon
the earth. And . . . I shall see God,
whom I shall see for myself!

Job 19:25-27, ESVB

created to live in this environment of freedom. We witnessed them living in the freedom of being transformed to their purpose of being a duck. While they had been living a life that seemed, at least at first, perfect (to us, anyway), it was not the life for which they were intended.

How Can I Be Redeemed?

When you become a Christian through the blood of Jesus, you are set free from the old way of life and given the resources to live in your new identity of being redeemed. As a Christian, there are numerous things you have in common with all other Christians: You have been given a new identity, you have been freed, and you are redeemed.

Through Jesus, you have been redeemed and freed from living your life in a way that is contradictory to God's intended purpose. As Christians, we are freed when we release our regrets for God to redeem. This is wonderful news for us, because, as Nicole C. Mullin says, our redeemer lives! (GMA Dove Awards, 2001). These words come from the book of Job in the Old Testament: "For I know that my Redeemer lives, and at the last he will stand upon the earth" (*ESVB*, 2001, Job 19: 25).

My desire for the clock radio is insignificant compared to God's desire to redeem you. He waited until the perfect time in history to pay the price for your redemption. With the clock radio, when I paid the price necessary for its redemption, it became mine. However, even though God paid the price necessary for your redemption, you will not become His until you decide to accept the price He paid for you. If you have never done so, would you now allow Jesus to become your savior? It can happen if you will simply repent of your sins, trust in Jesus as your savior, and ask God to redeem you:

If you confess with your mouth that Jesus is Lord and believe in your heart that God raised him from the dead, you will be saved. For with the heart one believes and is justified, and with the mouth one confesses and is saved. (*ESVB*, 2001, Romans 10:9-10)

#iamredeemed

NOTES

CHAPTER 4

I Am Adopted

I Am Adopted

"These girls need to see a puppy!" were the first words I ever said to my wife. Do you remember the first words you said to your spouse? If you are not married, do you think that is something you would remember? Many people can tell you where they met their spouses, while others remember when they met or who introduced them. Some may remember the time of the year they met. My hunch, however, is that most people don't remember the first words they said to their spouse. Why? Because, like me, you had no idea the person to whom you were speaking would go on to become your spouse.

The first thing I ever said to Theresa, my wife, was, "These girls need to see a puppy!" You might think that is a strange way to begin a conversation with someone you've never met. Let me explain.

I was working part-time as a sales clerk at Doctor Pet Center pet store at Metro Center Mall in Jackson, Mississippi. Theresa and her daughters, Maggie and Jill, had recently moved to town for a fresh start. On the evening we met, she and a girlfriend had planned to take her girls to the movies, but their plans did not work out. Fortunately for me, those were the days before cell phones, and she could not find her friend. As an alternative to the movies, she decided to take her girls to the mall. While there, she told them they might *possibly* get a goldfish.

Rather than a display window like the other stores in the mall, the entire front left side of this pet store was made into an enormous glass fish tank. It was designed to catch the attention of those passing by and potentially give them a reason to come into the store. On this particular day, it had been a somewhat slow, but normal, day at the pet store. I had no idea something that would alter the course of my life was about to happen.

I was standing, as was my habit, in my usual place by the fish tank at the entrance of the store, wishing for a customer. Suddenly, I noticed this beautiful woman with two girls looking at the fish. The fish tank had done its job! My mind began to race, but not about selling her a fish, or pet supplies, or even a (somewhat overpriced) pet. My only thought was how to have a conversation with this gorgeous woman.

So, I said, looking at her two girls, "These girls need to see a puppy!"

Without waiting for an answer, I turned, walking toward the puppy pen--knowing they would follow. As the girls and I faced a wall of pens full of happy, barking puppies, I asked, "Which one would you girls like to play with?"

My plan was to distract the girls with a puppy so I could have a conversation with this lovely woman. After finding a puppy to keep the girl's attention, we went to one of the "puppy petting rooms," where we began our conversation.

She later asked, "Why did you want to talk to a woman with two children?"

The answer seems strange, but in addition to looking like a model who stepped out of a fashion magazine, I told her, "There are times when you hear God speak, and this was one of those times. In my spirit, I immediately knew several things about you. I knew you were not married; you were not divorced; and strangely, that you did not smoke." The only possible explanation for knowing this about her was that God was speaking to me.

"God desires to take you into His family and give you all the privileges of being His own child."

Although I do remember the first words I said to her, I don't remember much of the ensuing conversation. However, I received confirmation about all three: She told me she was not married, she was not divorced, and she did not like smoking. What I also learned was she a widow of three years with two girls: Maggie, age 3, and Jill, age 5. She had recently moved from her hometown to try and get a fresh perspective and start in life. The one thing I do remember is, before we finished our conversation, I asked for her phone number.

She agreed to give it to me, and six months later, we were married. We immediately became a family of four. Fast forward five years, and I legally adopted Maggie and Jill, who officially became my girls. This was one of the most important, and most memorable, days in my life.

Theresa, Maggie, and Jill on our wedding day

It took some time to get ready for adoption day. When it finally arrived, I was so excited. Everything was in order, and the paperwork was complete. We all were dressed in our best and ready for our appointment at the attorney's office. What Theresa and the girls did not know was I had a big surprise planned for Maggie and Jill when the adoption was finalized. As soon as we signed the paperwork, the declaration was made that their last name was officially changed to my last name: Mitchell. That's when I said, "I have a little surprise for you girls."

Earlier that week at a sporting goods store, I had two sweatshirts made with the words, "I'm a Mitchell," printed on the front. I wanted the world to know that I not only gave them my heart, but I also gave them my name. They were my girls!

During the process of getting ready for the adoption, several surprising things happened. There were testimonies to gather and a remarkable amount of legal and background work to be done. The most amazing to me, though, was to find out when the adoption was finalized, their birth certificates would be changed to list me as their birth father. For all of history and long after we are gone, anyone searching their family tree will find only my name on their birth certificates.

What It Means To Be Adopted

In each chapter, the focus is to complete the statement, "I am..." by using words found in scripture to describe how God sees you. We have seen the Bible teaches that God sees us as chosen, forgiven, loved, and redeemed. In this chapter, we will find that God also sees us as adopted.

To understand what it means to be adopted by God, we can transfer our earthly understanding of adoption to a spiritual understanding. The earthly definition of adoption is, "a legal action by which a person takes into his family a child not his own for the purpose of treating him as and giving him all the privileges of his own child" (David, 2014, p. 61). From a heavenly perspective, God desires to take you into His family and give you all the privileges of being His own child. As earthly children benefit from their parents' resources, we share God's treasures as His children.

"For all God gives to His son Jesus is now ours too" (*The Living Bible*, 1971, Romans 8:17).

Of all the ways we have described how God sees us, perhaps the most difficult to grasp is "adopted." Although the Bible says Jesus is God's "only begotten son" (*KJB*, 1611/1987, John 3:16), you are also God's child *by adoption*. You are in His family, and He is your heavenly Father, because of one reason: He adopted you into His family.

Paul described it this way in Galatians:

> But when the fullness of time had come, God sent forth His Son, born of woman, born under the law, to redeem those who were under the law, so that we might receive adoption as sons. And because you are sons, God has sent the Spirit of His Son into our hearts, crying, "Abba! Father!" So you are no longer a slave, but a son, and if a son, then an heir through God. (*ESVB*, 2001, Gal 4:4-7)

Because God is spirit and we are human, there are many concepts about God we find incomprehensible (*ESVB*, 2001, John 4:24). One of these is the truth explained in scripture about God's relationship to time. He is eternal (*ESVB*, 2001, Isaiah 40:28), so He has no beginning, He always has been, and He will have no end. Therefore, He always will be. Yet for our benefit, He chooses to work in time (*ESVB*, 2001, John 1:1-2). The timeless God stepped into history at the perfect time, in the form of His son Jesus. He did this so He could become your heavenly Father and to make a way for you be adopted into His family.

> Long before He laid down earth's foundations, He had us in mind, had settled on us as the focus of His love, to be made whole and holy by His love. Long, long ago He decided to adopt us into His family through Jesus Christ. (*The Message Bible*, 2018, Eph. 1:4-6)

Long before He laid down earth's foundations, He had us in mind, had settled on us as the focus of His love, to be made whole and holy by His love. Long, long ago He decided to adopt us into His family through Jesus Christ.

Ephesians 1:4-6, The Message Bible

Adoption Through His Son

God's plan was to send His son Jesus to redeem us through His death. For those who are willing, His desire is that they be adopted into His family. The great I Am not only created everything in the universe, but He also created you in your mother's womb. For *you*, He sent His Son, opening the way for you to take on His name and be called His child (*ESVB*, 2001, Romans 9:26).

God used many methods of communication before Jesus came to give leadership and direction to mankind. For example, God spoke to Elijah through a still, small voice (1 Kings 19:11-13). When Jonah was in the belly of the fish, God spoke to him through his circumstances (Jonah 1-4). God spoke to Moses through a burning bush (Exodus 3:1-4) and to Gideon through a fleece (Judges 6:37-40). God even used a donkey to speak to Balaam (Numbers 22:28)! At times, He also spoke to His chosen recipient through an angel or in a dream.

Sometimes He even decided to speak in visions. But "when the fullness of time had come," God's message came through His own Son, Jesus (*ESVB*, 2001, Gal. 4:4). His message today is the same as it was then. He desires for you to be adopted into His family and for you to know Him as your Father.

But why would God send His son with this message to a sinful and rebellious people? That is a question believers and nonbelievers ask. By sending His Son, He desires to make His *why* completely clear. Why did He send Jesus to the earth? "To redeem those who were under the law, so that we might receive adoption as sons" (*ESVB*, 2001, Gal. 4:5).

Why is an important word. On the bottom of my computer are several messages on Post-it Notes™. They are there as constant reminders of leadership principles important to me. One has been there so long, the paper has lost its color and the ink used to write the words is faded. It is an important principle I have believed for a long time. On it are the words, "Lead with the 'why' before the 'what.'" Yes, *why* is an important word.

If you stop to think about it, "Why?" is a question we ask on a regular basis. Moms (and wives!) ask, "Why don't you pick up your clothes?" Dads ask, "Why don't I go fishing more often?" Parents ask their adult children, "Why don't you call?

If you type "Why?" into Google search, the autocomplete function will respond with the most searched questions that begin with "why?" These questions may be as simple as *why is the sky blue? why do dogs eat grass?* and *why do zebras have stripes?* They are also as varied as *why is Fortnite bad? why is keto bad?* and *why were graham crackers invented? Why* is a word we all use to find the real reason behind an action.

By sending Jesus to redeem us, God was clearly explaining His *why*. The reason Jesus came to the earth was so we might be adopted into His family!

Being adopted into His family comes with great benefits. When you are adopted into God's family, He gives you a new name to identify you--one of those is adopted.

In Acts 11, we read for the first time that followers of Jesus were called Christians. This would make sense if Jesus's last name was actually "Christ." After all, followers of Martin Luther are called Lutherans. However, it is important to know Jesus's last name is *not* Christ. He is *the* Christ, a word that means "messiah" (Merriam-Webster, n.d.-a) or "the expected king and deliverer" (Merriam-Webster, n.d.-b).

Therefore, as a follower of Jesus, you are called "Christian." This joins you to Him as a member of His family. The first time people were called Christians was because their behavior, speech, and lifestyle were like that of Jesus. Quite simply, they were identified by their familial characteristics.

Elias Bickerman (1986) better clarified the meaning of the name Christian. He said, "All these Greek terms, formed with the Latin suffix -*ianus* . . . express the idea that the men or things referred to, belong to the person to whose name the suffix is added" (p. 147).

Your new name, Christian, means you belong to God's family. However, that is not the only name connecting you to God's family. God identifies you by many names. Some of those names we have already discovered. He calls you by the name of forgiven, the name of loved, and the name of redeemed. God likewise says for those in heaven:

"I will also give that person a white stone with a new name written on it, known only to the one who receives it" (*ESVB*, 2001, Rev. 2:17).

You will receive a document, a "white stone," your adoption papers, with your family name inscribed on it, identifying you for all eternity as God's child.

God Is Your Guide

For even the most skeptical, the global positioning system, or GPS, has replaced the printed roadmap. If you need directions, you type your destination into your car or phone's GPS, and it gives you turn-by-turn directions. With its current technology, you would think the directions would be faultless. However, no matter how up-to-date

Siri or Alexa's directions might be, occasionally they take you to an unintended destination.

The good news is that God's directions are always clear. More importantly, His destination for you is crystal clear. God, your loving heavenly Father, guides His children on the right path of life. He sent His spirit to guide you. He will never give you wrong directions.

As His child, He also blesses you and frees you with His forgiveness "so you are no longer a slave" (*ESVB*, 2001, Gal. 4:7). It helps to understand the context of this statement. In biblical times, many people who had no other way of making a living would sell themselves into slavery. In the same way, when we have not become part of God's family, we are all slaves to sin. Fortunately for us, God emancipates His children from the bonds of sin by adoption.

Because He adopted you, you now have freedom from the pull of sin, as well as its results. You have complete freedom from the power of sin over your life. *The Message Bible* (2018) described it this way: "The spirit of life in Christ, like a strong wind, has magnificently cleared the air, freeing you from a fated lifetime of brutal tyranny at the hands of sin and death" (Romans 8:1-2).

To be adopted into God's family "means that the true and living God, the Creator of the heavens and the earth, by grace has made believers members of his family with all the rights and responsibilities that go with that status" (Ortlund, 2014, para. 4). How amazing and comforting it is to know God sees you as His own--adopted into His eternal family.

The Mitchell Family

When I adopted Jill and Maggie, Theresa and I received adoption papers, with my name as their father and their new name: Mitchell. This was proof to any who asked that we were a family. God also provides proof--in the form of a white stone--with your new name (one that only you and God will know). That is proof you are His adopted child. While people on Earth will be able to find my family's names associated with each other in the legal records, a time will come when those records will no longer exist. However, God's "adoption papers" will last throughout eternity. As excited as Theresa, our family, and I were when the girls officially became our children on adoption day, everyone who becomes a child of God should be even more excited--because even the angels rejoice on that day!

"Just so, I tell you, there is joy before the angels of God over one sinner who repents" (*ESVB*, 2001, Luke 15:10).

#iamadopted

Just so, I tell you, there is joy before the angels of God over one sinner who repents.

Luke 15:10, ESVB

NOTES

CHAPTER 5

I Am Accepted

I Am Accepted

"He's leaving (leaving), on that midnight train to Georgia (leaving on a midnight train)" (Weatherly, 1973). Sound familiar? Of course it does, unless you have been living on the planet Pluto since 1973. Gladys Knight and the Pips made "Midnight Train to Georgia" a timeless and universally recognized song.

Recently, my wife and I heard this song on a commercial, and I said, "Did I ever tell you the guy who wrote that song was my dad's secretary's son?"

As you can imagine, her response was, "What?!? You never told me that. No he wasn't."

"Yes, he was," was my answer. "It was Jimmy Weatherly from my hometown, Pontotoc, Mississippi. He was also a standout quarterback at Ole Miss, and it was originally called 'Midnight Train to Houston.'"

It took some convincing, but (after several internet searches) she said, "That is amazing! You are right!"

"Midnight Train to Georgia" may not be your favorite song, but if you had to choose, what would you say is your favorite song? When I was a teenager, and through young adulthood, music was playing if I was awake. What about you? Are you a music person? We could disagree about our favorite song, but I am certain we can agree music is another language that communicates no matter your native tongue.

Maybe you don't know a person . . . who knows a person . . . who is related to a person . . . who wrote a famous song, but do you recognize the name of singer/songwriter Shirley Ellis? No, it is not a trick question. I am not a gambler, but even if you do not recognize her name, I would bet you know at least one of her songs. Not only do you know it, but I would wager it is one you have had a fun time singing.

Shirley Ellis and Lincoln Chase wrote an unusual--and unusually popular--song almost 60 years ago called "The Name Game" (Ellis & Chase, 1964), also known as the "Banana Song" (Songfacts, n.d.). Although the song is almost universally known and sung, most people are not aware of the name of the writer or the singer. As I said, I believe you not only will recognize her song but, at some point in your life, you sang it.

Here is how to sing "The Name Game" song:

Using the name *Catie* as an example, the song follows this pattern:

> Catie, Catie, bo-batie,
> Banana-fanna fo-fatie
> Fee fi mo-matie
> Catie!

A verse can be created for any name with stress on the first syllable, with *X* as the name and *Y* as the name without the first consonant sound (if it begins with a consonant), as follows:

> (X), (X), bo-b (Y)
> Banana-fana fo-f (Y)
> Fee-fi-mo-m (Y)
> (X)!

> (The Name Game, 2021, "Rules")

I knew you knew a Shirley Ellis song! Can you rhyme and sing your name with "The Name Game" song? Everyone likes to hear their name in "The Name Game" song. It has been said there is no sweeter sound to a person than the sound of one's own name.

Before (or shortly after) you were born, your parents decided on your name. All of your life, your name identifies you and sets you apart from others. There are few things that can more indelibly describe you than your name.

Many times, as we go through life, we are given a nickname because of a characteristic or habit. Nicknames can be given by our friends--or sometimes by our enemies. Most of the time, nicknames are harmless, and we enjoy the notoriety they bring. My middle name is Ralph. I don't know when it began, or who was the first to say it, but at some point, I was given the nickname Rufus.

Nicknames as Labels

Sometimes, nicknames can be become a label, and a label can cause us to change how we see ourselves. Have you ever been labeled? Labels can quickly change how we see ourselves. They can build us up or break us down.

Maybe someone labeled you as smarty pants, stupid, slow as molasses, ugly as mud, or something even worse. Those names can radically alter how we see ourselves. No matter how hard you try to avoid the label, at times we begin to believe--and become--our labels. They change how we see ourselves. Some familiar people with labels are:

Billy the Kid
Conan the Barbarian
Doubting Thomas
Blackbeard the Pirate

When you begin to live like your label, the name game is no game. A label can lead to indulging in self-destructive behavior, putting up a façade, and being willing to do anything to stop the pain.

We all need to be reminded these labels have nothing to do with how God sees us. Our minds begin to think, *if they see me this way, then obviously it must be true. If this is true about me who would ever want to spend time with me?* As children, we are taught to say, *sticks and stones may break my bones, but words will never hurt me.* But we all know they can. They can bring feelings of isolation, loneliness, and depression. Fortunately, the reality is this: The way God sees you is the true you.

Whatever label you may be wearing, and however it is impacting the way you live, I am challenging you to see that God accepts you. Let Him give you a new view of yourself that is completely and totally accepted by Him. When you see yourself as accepted by God, you can begin to become who God says you are rather than your label.

No matter your label or how you see yourself today, God accepts you just as you are. There is nothing you could do that would make God accept you any more or less than He does right now. Just as there are few things about you more powerful than your name, there is nothing more powerful to give you strength to live every day than seeing yourself through the eyes of God as accepted.

To become the person the scripture says you are begins with hearing who you are not:

You are not the label
You are not what others think
You are not your past
You are not what you have done

I Am...

You ARE who God says you are! God boldly says to you, through the Apostle Paul, "No, in all these things we are more than conquerors" (*ESVB*, 2001, Romans 8:37). Whom are you going to believe? Whose voice are you going to trust? The One who created you, loves you, and accepts you just like you are, or are you going to believe and trust a different voice? God sees you as called to be on His side. He has chosen you and has plans for your life.

What Do Others Say About Us?

Some of the most difficult times to overcome in life are those times when the voice of those we respect say they see us as less than God sees us. Just remember: No matter the credentials of the voice speaking into your life, God's vision of your life always trumps any other voice.

I felt called to preach at the age of 15. About midway through my senior year of high school, each of my classmates had a meeting with our guidance counselor. In our small town, almost everyone knew everyone, so meeting with my guidance counselor was not meeting with a stranger. I knew him fairly well, and he knew me fairly well. He was a member and leader in our church, so I saw him almost every Sunday. His wife was great friends with my mom, so I saw him in our home. He was attending church the day I told our church family I felt called to be a pastor. He was aware I was meeting with our pastor each week to learn about a pastor's responsibilities.

Because of our relationship, when it was my turn to meet with him as my guidance counselor, I was excited. He asked, as he did with each student he met with that day, "What do you plan to do with your life?"

Eagerly I said, "As you know, God has called me to be a pastor. I have been looking forward to meeting today to see how you can help me know my next steps."

In my young mind, I saw him as an adult I respected. My belief was he would affirm what I was convinced was God's vision for my life. What he said next I could not believe.

He said, "Your grades are not that good, and your ACT score is not that strong. I heard you preach your first sermon, and you are not a very good speaker. Looking at your ability, you need to know college is for those who are more intelligent than you. God has more capable people than you that He can use. I think you need to consider doing something where you can make a living."

Feelings of confusion and rejection began to flood my mind. Was God's plan for my life actually to be a pastor? Had I misunderstood His leadership? Maybe my guidance counselor was right: I am not smart enough to go to college. What if I am not able to make it as a pastor? If who he says I am is really who I am, then he must be right. After all, he is the guidance counselor.

What do you do at this point? Scripture boldly asks about these times in life. In Paul's letter to the Romans, he asks this question: "What, then, shall we say in response to these things?" (*NIVB*, 1973, Romans 8:31a). Say to *what* things? The disbelief in our ability. The labels people give us. The doubt in our capacity to hear from God.

It is difficult for a mature believer to overcome negativity. For a teenager who was convinced I had clearly heard from God about His plan for my life, it was challenging to hear this doubtful prognosis from a respected adult, to say the least.

*If God is for us, who can be
against us?*

Romans 8:31b, NIVB

When those whom we respect say we can't do it, when those whom we love put us down, when those whom we admire say, "You will never make it," when those whose voices we are accustomed to following say they disagree with God's voice, how are we to respond? It is in these circumstances of life we must have a strong understanding of how God sees us and who He says we are. No matter what others assert or how they see us, Paul continues to provide the answer for us: "If God is for us, who can be against us?" (*NIVB*, 1973, Romans 8:31b). God sees us as accepted, and His view never changes.

What Do We Say About Ourselves?

What we say about ourselves can be just as challenging to overcome as what others say about us. Getting caught in the comparison trap also makes it difficult to maintain God's view of ourselves. As a pastor, I can tell you from experience that ministers also often struggle in this area. Pastors are not immune to the comparison trap. Seeing God bless another minister with success can cause a pastor to wonder, "Why is God not blessing me in the same way He is blessing that minister?" When we move our focus from what God says about us through scripture to what we begin to say about ourselves, our understanding of how God sees us can easily change.

As a pastor, I must constantly fight to overcome the comparison trap. No matter how significantly God may have blessed the ministry He is allowing me to lead, when I see other pastors building new buildings, their congregations rapidly growing, or God blessing a unique ministry, I begin to compare what they are achieving to what I have achieved. When I allow this to happen, feelings of, "I must not know as much as they do," "I guess I don't pray in faith like they do,"

"When you see yourself as accepted by God, you can begin to become who God says you are rather than your label."

"I'm not reading my Bible as consistently as they do," or "I just don't lead as well as they do," begin to grow. After all, if I did all of these things, then my ministry would be more successful, right?

How we feel about ourselves is often the result of unwise comparisons. The only way to overcome the comparison trap is to see ourselves the way God sees us. God sees you as accepted and, as so, He has equipped you with all the skill necessary to accomplish His specific plan for your life.

It is easy--and dangerous--for us to allow our views of ourselves to be filtered through the way we see others rather than how God sees us. Imagine you go to your friend's house, and it looks like it was decorated by the editors of *Southern Living* magazine. In the back of your mind, you are thinking, "My house looks like an exploded dorm room!" Or, you walk in, and their house smells like Bath and Body Works while yours reminds you of 12-year-old boys after a soccer game. The feelings of *I wish I could be like her* or *he always seems to have it together* begin to dominate.

The attack of the enemy continues. You post pictures on Facebook of your "staycation," and then you see your neighbors' pictures of their Hawaiian vacation. While posting, you notice you have 52 followers, and they have 2,952. You begin to ask, "What is wrong with me?" and the feelings of inadequacy caused by the comparison trap grow even stronger.

God's acceptance of you is not based on the cleanliness of your house or your Facebook followers. God accepts you because He loves you! He loves you because He created you. He created you to be specifically and uniquely you and not to be anyone else. He sees you as accepted as distinctively you.

There is no waiting period to be accepted by God. "Therefore, there is *now* [emphasis added] no condemnation at all for those who are in Christ Jesus" (*NIVB*, 1973, Romans 8:1). Now means today. Now means at this moment you have been pardoned from all your sins and have been given liberty and freedom to live your life as accepted by the creator of the universe.

As accepted, God has direction for your life. You don't have to try to live up to the standards others have for you or even those you impose on yourself. Your goal is to live out God's desires for you: "'For I know the plans I have for you,' declares the LORD, 'plans to prosper you and not to harm you, plans to give you hope and a future'" (*NIVB*, 1973, Jeremiah 29:11). When you follow God's plans, you find satisfaction and fulfillment because you are living up to His standards.

Winners and Losers

What is the opposite of a winner? A loser. We all know what it means when someone looks at us and holds their hand to their forehead making an L-sign with only their thumb and index finger extended. You are a loser! However, all the labels of the world and all the broken dreams and mistakes of life don't have the power to defeat you. In fact, God sees you as the opposite.

Because you are accepted by God, He sees you as a winner. The Apostle Paul asks us to imagine some of life's most difficult circumstances that cause people to feel defeated. You know, those times in life when it may seem like we are losing, like walking through the valley of the shadow of death, or struggling with mistakes of the past, or worrying over an uncertain future. Paul says, "But in all these things we overwhelmingly conquer through Him who loved us" (*NASB*, 1960, Romans 8:37). God does not want you to *make it through* life.

His plan is for you to *conquer* life. In ancient Greek, the word for conquer is *nikao*. Does it sound familiar? It means victor or winner. That is why the owners of the Nike shoe company chose that name. The implication is if you wear these shoes, you will be a winner. Paul says because God choose you, you are a winner.

The word Paul chooses to describe the victory of the believer over life's tallest obstacles is *hypernikomen* (Constable, 2021). It means a super victor. It means we can, "overcome any spiritual obstacle that the world or Satan puts in our way because **in all these things we overwhelmingly conquer through Him who loved us**" (MacArthur, 1991, p. 514). You are not just a medalist, a finisher, or top 10. You are a super winner! The idea is a winner who wins by such a margin that the competition is vanquished beyond recognition. You are a winner, not by a nose, but without question. The kind of victory this word describes is like the victory of Joshua at Jericho, the Israelites over the Egyptians at the Red Sea, David defeating Goliath, and Jesus's victory over death. Because God accepts you, you are in the winner's circle hall of fame!

Don't you dare believe what someone else says about you that is derogatory, limiting, or negative. Don't you dare believe what your inner-self says about you that reflects anything less than what God says about you. Let God give you a new view of you. You are accepted by God and a super winner.

For all of us, difficulties will come. However, to be an overcomer, you must have something to overcome. Living from God's view of being accepted means we can be victorious through even the most troublesome of life's circumstances. Your heavenly Father has equipped you to overcome your past, a rotten habit, or a bad reputation. It is easy to believe the worst. God wants you to believe the best. When He leads you to victory over these things, you become the *victor* not the *victim!*

Being accepted by your heavenly Father happens because Jesus's tomb is empty. He is the only one who can take your pain and turn it into healing, your sorrow and turn it into joy, and your mourning and turn it into dancing. Because you believe in Christ, you are accepted, and your best days are ahead.

Acceptance Comes With a Cost

Music is an important part of many people's lives, and worship music is no different. It can be the most favorite--or least favorite--portion of any church service. While you won't hear "The Name Game" (Ellis & Chase, 1964) or "Midnight Train to Georgia" (Weatherly, 1973) in churches, what you may hear are songs declaring what this chapter addresses--your acceptance. I have one more question for you: Are you familiar with Billy James Foote? This name may be even more obscure than Jimmy Weatherly or Shirley Ellis, but if you are a fan of contemporary Christian music, you may be familiar with his work. He recounted Jesus was condemned for you to be accepted:

"I'm forgiven because You were forsaken
I'm accepted, You were condemned
I'm alive and well, Your Spirit is within me
Because You died and rose again" (Foote, 1999).

Do you recognize it? It is the song, "You Are My King," also known as "Amazing Love." It was the number one song on the U.S. *Billboard* Christian Songs chart for the Newsboys in 2003 (Billboard, n.d.), but it was originally recorded by Phillips, Craig, and Dean in 2001 ("You Are My King," 2021) and many others since then. If you aren't familiar with the song, I recommend you search for it on YouTube--there are several very good recordings of it there.

"God does not want you to just make it through life. His plan is for you to conquer life."

I Am…

What does this mean to us? It means we are accepted--just as we are--by the King of Kings and the Lord of Lords. It also means we should be accepting of our brothers and sisters in Christ. In Paul's letter to the Romans, he stated it quite clearly: "Therefore, accept one another, just as Christ also accepted us, for the glory of God" (*NASB*, 1960, Romans 15:7).

#iamaccepted

# NOTES

CHAPTER 6

I Am Loved

I Am Loved

Is love enough? When people give expensive or extravagant gifts to express their love, many times it catches our attention. What is the greatest gift you have given to express your love? Was it anything like the $485 million, 86-carat Koh-i-noor diamond, given by the Maharaja of the Sikh Empire, Duleep Singh, to Queen Victoria (Dezman, 2021)? How about the $827 million Taj Mahal, given by Mughal Emperor Shah Jahan to his late wife, Mumtaz Mahal (Dezman, 2021)? For me, it was the engagement ring I gave my wife. Six months after we met, I was determined we were going to be married. So, I put a plan together to communicate my love. My plan included a marriage proposal and giving the most expensive gift I have ever given.

When I planned my proposal, the creativity of that event was limited to my imagination. Fortunately for those who are currently under pressure to have the perfect proposal, help is available. There are many websites, such as apracticalwedding.com, brides.com, and theknot.com, that offer a multitude of proposal suggestions. See if any of the suggestions below are ways in which you would "pop the question"--or ways in which you would like to be asked.

One of those suggestions is to hire an airplane skywriter to write out your proposal (Hill, 2020). Another is to spell out, "Will you marry me?" in refrigerator magnets (Hill, 2020). You could also hire a choir or band to play your future spouse's favorite love song so you can pop the question (Hill, 2020). These proposal ideas are even rated on a 1-to-5 scale for cost and effort. As you can see, the jitters of proposing are only increased by the pressure of it also being romantically creative.

Will She Say Yes?

Although I did not feel as pressured as many do to plan an "over-the-top" engagement proposal, I still wanted it to be a perfectly memorable event. After saving, saving, and saving some more, I took all the money I had in the world to the very finest jeweler in our city and began to shop for the perfect ring. It was there I learned that the letter C may be a woman's favorite letter in the alphabet--have you ever heard of <u>c</u>ut, <u>c</u>olor, <u>c</u>larity, and <u>c</u>arats? After making a very difficult decision and with the best ring I could afford in hand, it was now time to develop a proposal plan.

To be honest, it was not very original, but my plan was to propose at the best and most romantic restaurant I could afford (a difficult task after spending so much on the ring!). After a little research for the perfect place, I made reservations at a restaurant suggested to be excellent: Ruth's Chris Steak House. Neither of us had ever been to restaurant like this--a restaurant that catered to your every need. When we got there, we were in wide-eyed amazement. Much to my personal delight, as we were escorted to our table, my senses were overwhelmed with the lighting, decorations, and smells. Walking past other patrons, I tried to read my future wife's facial expressions and body language to see if she was as impressed as I was. To my relief, it seemed like my plan was coming together!

When we were seated, our waiter handed each of us a menu. My nervousness immediately increased tenfold! For two people who would normally *share* a Happy Meal' on a date, to say the prices were breathtaking for both of us is an understatement! After I spent several minutes assuring her we would not have to wash dishes to pay our bill, we placed our order. My research paid off--not only was the ambience extremely romantic, the meal was outstanding!

What my bride did not know was, just after being seated, I had a conversation with the maître d' (while on a decoy trip to the restroom). I nervously left the gift-wrapped engagement ring, the most expensive gift I had ever given, with this total stranger. I described my plan and, with a slight smile, he happily agreed to help me put my plan into action.

During my research, a friend told me "after your meal, your waiter will bring a big tray of desserts by your table." He then said, "Whatever you do, *do not* order dessert!" He said this because, when offering the desserts, the waiter does not tell you the cost. He was speaking from experience. While trying to impress a girlfriend, he made the mistake of ordering a dessert. In his words, his single piece of cake was, "as expensive as four cakes at a bakery."

As I explained to the maître d', my plan was, after our meal, to have the waiter bring the dessert tray by. On the tray, along with the desserts, would be the gift-wrapped engagement ring. I was told this would not be a problem--the night was going perfectly! We finished our meal and, on cue, the waiter came by and asked, "Would you like to see our dessert tray?" With the menu prices still on her mind, Theresa immediately but graciously said, "No, thank you." Then looking at me, she softly said, "How could you possible want dessert after such a perfect meal?"

What was I to do now? The most important part of my plan was in danger of not being executed. Looking at the waiter, I quickly said, "You are right, but let's at least take a look." Without waiting for further discussion, the waiter was off to get the dessert tray. The plan was still on track!

Within a moment, he was back with a tray filled with four of the most beautifully decorated desserts you can imagine, and in the middle of the tray was the gift-wrapped box. Looking at Theresa, he said, "Do you see anything you might like?" She looked at me, back at him, and she reached for the box. When she opened it, and I said, "Will you marry me?" she immediately said, "YES." All these years later, when we finish a meal, she will look at me, bat her eyes, and inquisitively ask, "Do you think I should order dessert?" I guess my plan for a memorable proposal worked!

God's Love vs. Human Love

I knew I loved my wife before I proposed. I also know she was aware of this love. However, I needed to express my love to her in a way that could not be questioned. In the same way, God's love without expression was not enough. He could not contain it; He had to display- -in an unforgettable way--His love for you. Since God created the world, He has put together an extravagant plan to express His love for you.

Undeniably the most familiar verse in the Bible is a declaration of God's demonstration of love for you: "For God so loved the world, that he gave his only Son, that whoever believes in him should not perish but have eternal life" (*ESVB*, 2001, John 3:16). Simply put, when God sees you, He sees you as worthy of His demonstration of love.

This timeless verse gives refreshing encouragement to parents who are helping their children begin to understand their identities in Christ as identities of being loved. It motivates students who are choosing to live out their identities as believers who are loved. It offers guidance for adults who are choosing to agree that God sees them as loved. It also affirms the senior generation who set the example of what it looks like to live their lives loved by God.

Maybe the best way to understand God's personalized love for you from John 3:16 is to replace *the world* with your name. Imagine the verse with your name in it instead: "For God so loved (your name), that He gave His only son . . . ."

The Greek word for *world* is kósmos (n.d.), and one of its definitions is "the ungodly multitude" (Church of the Great God, n.d., def. 6). This is the world God loved. It doesn't say that God loved all the good guys. Or that God loved all the Jews. Or that God loved all the saints. The world God loves is broken. He loves it with all that is wrong with it, without exception. John clearly says, "God so loved the world," and when it says *world*, that leaves no one out, including you.

Think about God's love for you this way. John, God's inspired writer under the Holy Spirit's direction not only wrote, "God so loved the world," he described God's big love for you by using the little adjective "so." The purpose of that little adjective is to emphasize the amount of God's love for you. "God *so* loved" implies God *extremely* loved, *remarkably* loved, and *unconditionally* loved the world. In describing His love as being for the whole world, it includes and specifically means God loves you.

Christian author Max Lucado (1996) writes:

> If God had a refrigerator, your picture would be on it. If he had a wallet, your photo would be in it. He sends you flowers every spring and a sunrise every morning. Whenever you want to talk, he'll listen. He can live anywhere in the universe, and he chose your heart. And the Christmas gift he sent you in Bethlehem? Face it, friend. He's crazy about you! ("Chapter One," para. 22)

"The only people Jesus ever invited to follow Him were sinners."

This Is How Much God Loves You

Biblical love is about doing, not about feeling. God's love for you is a demonstration of how much He loves you. Have you seen someone outstretch their arms as wide as possible and say, "This is how much I love you"? Don't you think God did that when the arms of Jesus were stretched out on a Roman cross for you? God's word not only *says* He loves you, He *demonstrates* His love for you by giving His Son.

For us, finding the perfect gift to demonstrate our love can be challenging. There are some amazing gifts created with the intention of "wowing" the recipient. For example, I recently discovered you can purchase 24-carat gold shoelaces for $20,000. For those who insist on only the best in cleaning equipment, you can purchase a gold-plated vacuum priced at $1 million. For animal lovers, you might be interested in the gift of a 52-carat diamond dog collar valued at $3.2 million.

However, no matter the extravagance of our gifts, they are insignificant when compared to God's gift to the world: the demonstration of His love for us offered through Jesus. God gave His son to demonstrate, prove, and display how much He loves us: "He who did not spare his own Son, but gave him up for us all" (*ESVB*, 2001, Romans 8:32).

When the Bible says God loves whoever believes in him, that is proof of His love for you and God's validation of your worth to Him. God did not send Jesus to rebuke you; He sent Him to rescue you. Jesus didn't come to criticize you; He came to cleanse you. He didn't come to punish you; He came to pardon you. He didn't come to destroy you; He came to deliver you.

"If God had a refrigerator, your picture would be on it."

Max Lucado

Will You Accept God's Gift?

I realize many people do not want to think about this, but when John wrote, "whoever believes in him will not perish" (*ESVB*, 2001, John 3:16), the implication is there are those who *will* perish. The truth is we are all eternal beings. We will all spend eternity in one of two places: Heaven or Hell. God's love gives all of us the opportunity to spend that eternity with Him--in Heaven.

Rest assured, God does not send anyone to Hell. The Bible plainly says: "If you confess with your mouth that Jesus is Lord and believe in your heart that God raised Him from the dead, you will be saved" (*ESVB*, 2001, Romans 10:9). When a person chooses to reject God's offer of love and reject Jesus, that person is choosing to spend eternity separated from God's love.

To spend eternity in Hell is a choice, just as trusting in God's gift of Jesus is a choice. The only people in Hell are those who turned away from His great love for them. All of them said, "No, thank you," to the offer of the gift of eternal life in Heaven through Jesus.

Someone might say, "I cannot believe a loving God would send someone to Hell." However, making this statement of disbelief is also making a statement of belief. The statement says there is a God, He is loving, and there is a place some people go called Hell. Ultimately, everything God does is an expression of His love, and the only reason people go to Hell is because they refuse to accept God's love for them.

In Hell, hope perishes. Happiness is nonexistent. Optimism dies. Kindness is absent. Peace expires. The Bible describes Hell as a place of blackest darkness, everlasting destruction, and where there is weeping and gnashing of teeth. It is also referred to as the pit, a place of torment, and as the lake of fire. It is where those who choose to reject God's offer of love perish.

God's plan for you is that you avoid life's greatest mistake by accepting life's greatest gift to meet your greatest need. Life's greatest gift is eternal life. Through Jesus, God offers you the gift of eternal life. Every drop of blood He spilled was on purpose. One of those drops has your name on it, making it possible for you to accept life's greatest gift. Because of His love for us, God gave out of His extravagant resources; He gave His only Son to meet our greatest need.

If you still don't feel like you are worthy of being loved by God, know that the only people Jesus ever invited to follow Him were sinners. As sinners, Jesus is God's offer to us to avoid life's greatest mistake. Life's greatest mistake is to choose to reject God's love and spend eternity separated from Him.

A Misunderstanding

When our son, Noah, was about five, he was having a discussion with my wife's boss, Joe, who is a huge Disney fan. He had recently returned from a four-day trip to Disney World. Rather than drive the 14 hours from his home to Orlando, he decided to fly.

As they talked, Noah's eyes lit up: His attention hung on Joe's every word as he began to describe his trip to Disney World. Joe was so kind and patient to answer all of this five-year-old's questions of curiosity. Noah seemed interested in hearing about Disney, but as Joe would begin to describe a portion of the Magic Kingdom, Noah would ask a question about the flight. He was mesmerized by the aspects of flying.

So, with a smile, Joe began to describe the flight in detail. He explained the check-in process, finding his seat, the seatbelt announcement, and the offer of a soft drink and peanuts. In the corner of the room where they were talking, Noah noticed a tall, skinny cardboard box with the airline's logo. It was a courtesy box provided by the airline to protect Joe's hang-up bag.

For God so loved the world, that he gave his only Son, that whoever believes in him should not perish but have eternal life.

John 3:16, ESVB

Noah asked, "What is in this big box?"

Joe said, "That's what they put my clothes in when I got on the plane."

You could see his expression change from one of intrigue to one of sincere worry. After a moment of hesitation, Noah slowly asked, with all the innocence of a five-year-old, "You don't wear clothes while you are on the airplane?"

Just as with Noah and the airline box, when we talk about Hell, there is a lot of misunderstanding. But rest assured--God's plan is to clarify your choice for you.

The greatest gift ever offered is God's gift of eternal life. Jesus is God's offer to gain that life. You simply need to accept the gift of Jesus to spend eternity with Him in Heaven. "For God so loved the world, that he gave his only Son, that whoever believes in him should not perish but have eternal life" (*ESVB*, 2001, John 3:16).

#iamloved

NOTES

CHAPTER 7

I Am . . .

I Am...

It was a dark and stormy night. Actually, it wasn't. It was a bluebird day. Clouds were drifting along by a soft breeze in the baby-blue sky. You could feel the warmth of the beaming sun. My son, Luke, and I were at Central Hills Baptist Retreat. We were there for a father/son Royal Ambassador weekend outing. Looking back, I now know a storm was the only thing that would have allowed us to avoid what the night would bring.

Luke and I had a fantastic day. It began with an early-morning horseback trail ride. Next, we took our turn in a very competitive target shooting competition with .22 rifles. After a typical camp lunch of sandwiches and bug juice, we made our way to the small lake. Putting on our life jackets, we launched our canoe and paddled until our arms felt like Jell-O™. Exhausted and tired, we decided we would cool off from the afternoon heat with snowballs from the Snack Shack. Although it had been a great day, I had no idea about what we were going to face.

As the sun began to set, we joined the other sons and dads from our group for evening worship. Luke had been waiting for this moment all day. Not for worship, but for worship to be over--so we could return to our tent for the night.

When we arrived at camp, the staff helped each father and son to their accommodations. Some years ago, the camp purchased Army-surplus puptents. This is where we would spend the night.

These were drab green tents with no bottom, no screens, and (obviously) no electricity. The tents were held up by two tall poles in the middle on either end and four shorter poles at each corner. The ropes for each pole were tied to stakes in the ground.

What we did not understand when we dropped our gear off at the tent earlier that day was we would have guests joining us for the night. Immediately, when darkness fell, our tent was filled by the unwanted guests: a swarm of gigantic mosquitoes!

It was a sweltering hot night with humidity near 100%. The only air moving in the tent was from the flutter of mosquito wings. It seemed the mosquitoes' mission was twofold: One group had the responsibility of buzzing around your head near your ears and the other group attacked any exposed skin.

I determined the only way to survive the night was to pull the top of my sleeping bag over my head and hope and pray for morning. Sometime long after midnight, I finally drifted off to sleep. But it was short lived: Soon after going to sleep, I was awakened. This time, it was not the mosquitoes keeping me from sleep but a bright light. Luke was standing by my bed with his flashlight shining in my face. He said, "Dad? . . . Dad? . . . Are you awake? . . . Is that you?"

The preceding chapters have been written as a wakeup call so you might recognize the real you, the identity from which God intended for you to live. Much like Luke's flashlight when he wasn't sure if I was with him, their purpose is to be a light shining on your life, allowing the bright light of scripture to plainly illuminate who you are, enabling you to say with confidence, "Yes, that is me!"

With divine wisdom, God gives us His word with living illustrations of people--just like you and me--who have struggled to see themselves as God sees them. Throughout scripture, God gives us multiple examples of people whose self-perception was changed after an encounter with God and were able to say, "Yes, that is me; I am who God says I am."

I Am...

Whatever darkness has kept you from accepting the identity God has given you, I pray God makes these real-life examples lead you to a point of saying, "Yes, God, I can--and I do--see myself as you see me."

I Am Chosen

Your self-perception is not a limitation for what God has planned for your life. God does not evaluate people on their human characteristics or ability.

When you see yourself as only what you see in the mirror, or what you think of your human abilities, you often miss what God is doing or what He desires to do through you. God is concerned with the heart and what the Holy Spirit is allowed to do in your life.

Whatever excuse or fear or doubt you have will be overcome when you release it to God. Anything you consider to be a weakness will be transformed into a spiritual weapon when you allow God to work through you.

Just like many great Bible characters, you have been chosen by God. Have confidence in knowing God chose to create you so you might daily reveal His image to those around you, even using what you might consider a limitation. Because God chose you, just like so many other heroes of faith, you can also say, "Yes, that is me. I am chosen."

I Am Forgiven

We all need forgiveness. Sometimes we need it more than once for an offense we habitually commit. Many times, in those areas of great struggle, we make a promise: "God, I will never do that again."

We have all made commitments to God that we have broken. If you could physically see the face of Jesus after you broke your commitment to Him, what do you think His expression would be? Even though you might read disappointment on His face, would He still offer forgiveness?

If you are a Christian, I am sure your commitment to Jesus was genuine when you made your salvation decision. Your plan was to live for Jesus with all possible boldness in the face of even the most difficult challenge.

A repetitive sin, and one you make a vow you will never commit again, is one of the most difficult failures in life to come back from.

Because of Jesus's work on Calvary and your faith in Him, you can also say, "Yes, that is me. I am forgiven." Your faith in Jesus gives you the confidence to say you are forgiven. You can boldly live your life as a beacon that shows others: God chose to prove His love by offering me complete and total forgiveness. God's book of forgiveness, the Bible, contains almost 800,000 words that describe His forgiveness for you (The Bible Answer, 2018).

I Am Redeemed

Because of Jesus's work on Calvary and your faith in Him, you can also now say, "Yes, that is me. I am what I am, and I am redeemed." You can join Big Daddy Weave, and sing, "I am redeemed, You set me free, So I'll shake off these heavy chains, wipe away every stain, now I'm not who I used to be I am redeemed, I'm redeemed" (Weaver & Cowart, 2012).

What about your heavy chains? What false self-impression is Satan trying to use to weigh you down? It may be that your past life is a memory that you cannot escape. A portion of the reason God gives us examples of believers struggling in scripture is for us to see it is possible to move beyond our previous mistakes.

Part of the reason God gives us examples of struggling believers in scripture is for us to see it is possible to move past our past. No matter how far away from God you were before salvation, once you become a Christian, He never sees the old you. Even when we begin to doubt the transformation we know to be true through experience, He constantly reminds us we are His, and He has redeemed us.

John describes it this way: "For whenever our heart condemns us, God is greater than our heart, and He knows everything" (*ESVB*, 2001, 1 John 3:20).

As we see from that verse, when you are at your lowest moment, when you are thinking the worst of yourself, when your guilt is overwhelming, and when your remorse is strongest, God is greater than your doubts and fears. This means His vision of who you *are* always trumps who you *were*. You are now redeemed.

I Am Adopted

What is your name? What is your family name? Because of Jesus's work on Calvary and your faith in Him, you can now say, "Yes, that is me. I am a Christian. I am adopted."

God is greater than our heart, and He knows everything.

1 John 3:20, ESVB

If you remember, I adopted my daughters Jill and Maggie. For all of us to become a family, we followed a legal process, filled with paperwork and process steps. Once completed, Jill, Maggie, Theresa, and I were a family in the eyes of the world. The same process is available for you, if you choose to adopt someone into your family. However, there are some important differences between what adoptive families do and what God has done for you.

Quite simply, God did the impossible. The immortal God adopted *you*, a *mortal*, into His family for eternity. Through the process of adoption, you now have all the rights and privileges of His child. When you feel you are not worthy, just remember God paid the price necessary for you to be adopted into His forever family.

I Am Accepted

If you Google the word, "nerd," his picture is one of the first you will see. Although it has been more than 30 years since we were first introduced to the character of Steve Urkel and his famous line, "Did I do that?" his is the image that comes to mind when the word nerd is mentioned (Bickley et al., 1989-1998).

No matter how hard he tried, he could never convince the Winslow family to see him as anything other than an annoying neighbor (Bickley et al., 1989-1998). Although the Winslow family, at no time, saw Urkel for who he was, the writers of the show portrayed him in a way that the audience saw him for who he truly was: a loving, kind person who, like almost everyone else, is trying his best to have friends and navigate through the issues of life. Maybe he was so popular because all of us can see a little bit of ourselves in Steve Urkel.

"Part of the reason God gives us examples of struggling believers in scripture is for us to see it is possible to move past our past."

Just remember this: You do not have to try to impress God for Him to accept you. He accepts you as you are. Not only does scripture tell us God accepts you, He proved it by allowing Jesus to die for you. Quite simply, God is bigger than our biggest sense of rejection.

We are all on a spiritual journey. On this journey, God desires to build you up and not pull you down. He wants to lift your countenance, not make you depressed. His plan is to *en*courage you, not *dis*courage you. We may count ourselves out, but God counts us in. Because of Jesus's work on Calvary and your faith in Him, you can now say, "Yes, that is me. I am accepted by God."

I Am Loved

Were you ever the favorite? Were you momma's boy, daddy's girl, or the teacher's pet? As seen in previous examples, scripture says Jesus also has a favorite, and His favorite is you! The three words you long to hear, "I love you," are expressed from God to you. The most familiar verse in the Bible describes God's universal love: "For God so loved the world . . . ." (*ESVB*, 2001, John 3:16). But did you know this verse is also personal? God not only loves the world, He specifically loves you: "In this is love: not that we have loved God but that He loved us" (*ESVB*, 2001, 1 John 4:10).

God backs up what He says in His word through demonstrations of His love. Multiple times in scripture, we see God demonstrating His love. He demonstrated His love to the woman at the well, who was trying to find her identity through a man (*ESVB*, 2001, John 4:7-42). He demonstrated His love to a prostitute who washed his feet (*ESVB*, 2001, Luke 7:36-50), to the demon-possessed man of the Gadarenes (*ESVB*, 2001, Matt. 8:28-34), and to Thomas when he doubted Jesus was alive after the resurrection (*ESVB*, 2001, 20:24-29). As you can

In this is love: not that we have loved God but that He loved us.

1 John 4:10, ESVB

see, it does not matter what you have done: God loves you, which means you can say, "Yes, that is me. I am loved by God."

Those who study human interaction say for every negative encounter, it takes almost six to counterbalance it (Zenger & Folkman, 2013). God's love for humanity is mentioned hundreds of times across the pages of every book in the Bible. When it is darkest, God's light of love comes shining through.

God demonstrates how the greatest expression of affection is communicated: by focusing on the other person. He is focused on you!

I Am . . .

My hope is this book has been a spiritual aid to help you see yourself through the eyes of God. God knows all there is to know about you. The great songwriter of the Old Testament, David, wrote well over a hundred psalms about how intimately God knows you. Even knowing every detail about your life--past, present, and future--God *still* loves you! As you read the 139th Psalm, know it is all about God's love for you.

Psalm 139

> [1] You have searched me, LORD, and you know me.
> [2] You know when I sit and when I rise; you perceive my thoughts from afar.
> [3] You discern my going out and my lying down; you are familiar with all my ways.
> [4] Before a word is on my tongue you, LORD, know it completely.

⁵ You hem me in behind and before, and you lay your hand upon me.

⁶ Such knowledge is too wonderful for me, too lofty for me to attain.

⁷ Where can I go from your Spirit? Where can I flee from your presence?

⁸ If I go up to the heavens, you are there; if I make my bed in the depths, you are there.

⁹ If I rise on the wings of the dawn, if I settle on the far side of the sea,

¹⁰ even there your hand will guide me, your right hand will hold me fast.

¹¹ If I say, "Surely the darkness will hide me and the light become night around me,"

¹² even the darkness will not be dark to you; the night will shine like the day, for darkness is as light to you.

¹³ For you created my inmost being; you knit me together in my mother's womb.

¹⁴ I praise you because I am fearfully and wonderfully made; your works are wonderful, I know that full well.

¹⁵ My frame was not hidden from you when I was made in the secret place, when I was woven together in the depths of the earth.

¹⁶ Your eyes saw my unformed body; all the days ordained for me were written in your book before one of them came to be.

¹⁷ How precious to me are your thoughts, God! How vast is the sum of them!

¹⁸ Were I to count them, they would outnumber the grains of sand--when I awake, I am still with you.
(*NIVB*, 1973)

Would you ask God to use these verses as His bright light, shining on you as a wakeup call to live in the reality of who He says you are?

I Am...

When you see yourself through the eyes of God, hope for a brighter tomorrow will begin to voluntarily grow in your life like wildflowers in the spring.

We all have cheerleaders in our lives--those who boost our spirits. Many times, we are encouraged by the voice of our boss, our parents, our preacher, or by a teacher or a coach. However, there is no better feeling than hearing the voice of God definitively declare everything He has done for you.

Because of who God is, you have been chosen, forgiven, redeemed, adopted, accepted, and loved. With all of those blessings, and all of the verses in the Bible that tell you how much you mean to the God of the universe, you can now say, "I am . . . *me*. I can see myself as God sees me."

#iam

"Scripture says Jesus also has a favorite, and His favorite is you!"

NOTES

REFERENCES

Around the NFL Staff. (2021, May 4). *2021 NFL Draft was third most-watched draft ever.* https://www.nfl.com/news/2021-nfl-draft-was-third-most-watched-draft-ever

Associated Press. (2021, May 5). NFL draft drew 160,000 in Cleveland with protocols for limited attendance. *Cleveland.com.* https://www.cleveland.com/news/2021/05/nfl-draft-drew-160000-in-cleveland-with-protocols-for-limited-attendance.html

The Bible Answer. (2018, August 29). *How many words are in the Bible?* https://thebibleanswer.org/how-many-words-in-bible/

Bickerman, E. J. (1986). *Studies in Jewish and Christian history* (Pt. 3). E. J. Brill.

Bickley, W., Boyett, R. L., Miller, T. L. (Executive Producers). (1989-1998). *Family matters* [TV series]. Bickley-Warren Productions, Lorimar Television; Miller/Boyett Productions, Warner Bros. Television.

Billboard. (n.d.). *Hot Christian songs: The week of December 20, 2003.* https://www.billboard.com/charts/christian-songs/2003-12-20

Butler, T. C. (Ed.). (1991). *Holman Bible dictionary.* Holman Reference.

Callis, J., & Mayo, J. (2021, July 12). Draft day 1: Pick-by-pick rundown, analysis. *MLB.com.* https://www.mlb.com/news/2021-mlb-draft-day-1-complete-coverage

Carpenter, C. (n.d.) Overcomer *asks critical question: What do you allow to define you?* Christian Broadcasting Network. https://www1.cbn.com/movies/overcomer-asks-critical-question-what-do-you-allow-define-you

Church of the Great God. (n.d.). *Greek/Hebrew definitions: Kósmos.* https://www.bibletools.org/index.cfm/fuseaction/Lexicon.show/ID/G2889/kosmos.htm

Constable, T. L. (2021). *Notes on Romans.* https://planobiblechapel.org/tcon/notes/pdf/romans.pdf

Contemporary English Version Bible. (1995). Bible Gateway. https://www.biblegateway.com

David, H. (2014). *Acorn to an oak.* Westbow Press.

Dezman, C. (2021, July 14). 20 most expensive gifts ever given and how much they cost. *Byliner.* https://byliner.com/20-most-expensive-gifts-ever-given-and-how-much-they-cost/

Ellis, S. M., & Chase, L. (1964). *The name game* [Song]. Congress Records.

English Standard Version Bible. (2001). Bible Gateway. https://www.biblegateway.com

Foote, B. J. (1999). *You are my king (Amazing love)* [Song]. EMI CMG Publishing.

GMA Dove Awards. (2001). *Nicole C. Mullen--Redeemer* [Video]. YouTube. https://www.youtube.com/watch?v=DN8BmdFFfKI

Harrison, R. (Executive Producer). (2012-2019). *Pawn stars* [TV series]. Leftfield Pictures for History Channel.

Hill, S. (2020, July 13). *66 proposal ideas to spark romance*. https://www. theknot.com/content/romantic-ways-to-propose

IMDb. (2019). *Overcomer*. https://www.imdb.com/title/tt8186318/?ref_ =ttfc_fc_tt

International Standard Version Bible. (2014). Bible Gateway. https:// www.biblegateway.com

Kendrick, A. (Director). (2019). *Overcomer* [Film]. Affirm Films, in association with Provident Films.

King James Bible. (1611/1987). Bible Gateway. https://www. biblegateway.com

Kósmos. (n.d.). In *Google translate: English - detected* → *Greek*. https://translate.google.com/?sl=auto&tl=el&text=world&op= translate&hl=en

The Living Bible. (1971). Bible Gateway. https://www.biblegateway.com

Lucado, M. (1996). *Prayer: A heavenly invitation*. https://maxlucado. com/prayer-a-heavenly-invitation/

MacArthur, J. F. (1991). *The MacArthur New Testament commentary* (Vol. 15, Romans 1-8). Moody Publishers.

Merriam-Webster. (n.d.-a). Christ. In *Merriam-Webster.com dictionary*. Retrieved May 5, 2022, from https://www.merriam-webster.com/ dictionary/Christ

Merriam-Webster. (n.d.-b). Messiah. In *Merriam-Webster.com dictionary*. Retrieved May 5, 2022, from https://www.merriam-webster.com/ dictionary/messiah

Merriam-Webster. (n.d.-c). Theocracy. In *Merriam-Webster.com dictionary*. Retrieved May 5, 2022, from https://www.merriam-webster.com/dictionary/theocracy

The Message Bible. (2018). Bible Gateway. https://www.biblegateway.com

The name game. (2021, March 26). In *Wikipedia*. https://en.wikipedia.org/wiki/The_Name_Game

NBA.com Staff. (2021, July 31). 2021 NBA draft results: Picks 1-60. https://www.nba.com/news/2021-nba-draft-results-picks-1-60

New American Standard Bible. (1960). Bible Gateway. https://www.biblegateway.com

New International Version Bible. (1973). Bible Gateway. https://www.biblegateway.com

NFL.com. (n.d.). Trevor Lawrence. https://www.nfl.com/prospects/trevor-lawrence/32004c41-5751-4099-56fc-f565c8d26c06

Ortlund, G. (2014, October 13). *Adopted by the living God*. The Gospel Coalition. https://www.thegospelcoalition.org/article/adopted-by-the-living-god/

Songfacts. (n.d.). The name game. https://www.songfacts.com/facts/shirley-ellis/the-name-game

Weatherly, J. D. (1973). *Midnight train to Georgia* [Song]. Bibo Music Publishing.

Weaver, M. D., & Cowart, B. (2012). *I am redeemed* [Lyrics]. https://www.azlyrics.com/lyrics/bigdaddyweave/redeemed.html

Williams, H., Jr. (1996). Are you ready for some football? [Song]. On *ABC Monday Night Football: Official party album*. Hollywood Records.

You are my king (Amazing love). (2021, January 21). In *Wikipedia*. https://en.wikipedia.org/wiki/You_Are_My_King_(Amazing_Love)

Zenger, J., & Folkman, J. (2013, March 15). The ideal praise-to-criticism ratio. *Harvard Business Review*. https://hbr.org/2013/03/the-ideal-praise-to-criticism

04089992-00836057

Printed in the United States
by Baker & Taylor Publisher Services